In Defense of Creation

The Nuclear Crisis and a Just Peace

The
United
Methodist
Council of
Bishops

Foundation Document

 Graded Press

"Blessed are the peacemakers . . . ."
(Matthew 5:9)

Contents

Preface

"We write in defense of creation. We do so because the creation itself is under attack. Air and water, trees and fruits and flowers, birds and fish and cattle, all children and youth, women and men live under the darkening shadows of a threatening nuclear winter."

With these words the Council of Bishops challenges the people called United Methodist to enter into a period of prayerful reflection upon the nuclear arms crisis.

The *Pastoral Letter* and *Foundation Document* emerge from two years of study by the Council of Bishops. As bishops of the church, we make no attempt to "speak the mind of the church" on nuclear disarmament. We speak as pastors of the church to the church.

We are convinced, as the *Discipline* of our church says, that:

"The people of God [the laity] are the Church made visible in the world. It is they who must convince the world of the reality of the gospel or leave it unconvinced. . . . the Church is either faithful as a witnessing and serving community, or it loses its vitality and its impact on an unbelieving world."

(*The Book of Discipline, 1984*, ¶107)

Our purpose is to encourage and equip our members to become knowledgeable witnesses to the power of God in Christ to bring peace to the human family. We hope the United Methodist people will overcome their "nuclear numbness," find their voices, and speak and act for nuclear disarmament. Einstein said upon the advent of the nuclear age: "A new type of thinking is essential if mankind is to survive. . . ." Caring Christian people who are in touch with the vision of God for *shalom* can offer that new way of thinking.

Why is the Council of Bishops taking this initiative at this moment in history? We were startled by new scientific data that shows a nuclear interchange may have even more grave consequences for the future of the human family than we knew. Body counts in the tens of millions, millions more wounded, cities and civilizations lying in ruins have long been seen as the price of nuclear war. But from a meeting of some one hundred physicists, biologists, and atmospheric scientists in Washington, DC, came even more distressing news. These specialists spoke of incredible fire storms that would burn stored chemicals and fill the air with poisonous fumes. Within a week after a nuclear war, hundreds of tons of sooty smoke would absorb so much of the sun's rays that only five percent of the normal amount of light would reach the earth. Photosynthesis would be choked off. Virtually all land plants would be damaged or destroyed in the Northern Hemisphere. Every higher organism would risk starvation. The smoke would make temperatures plummet for several months, freezing surface waters to a depth of three feet. All biological life on planet earth would be gravely threatened.

So much evidence points to a runaway technological obsession that leads us inexorably toward that doomsday. As George F. Kennan put it, the superpowers proceed with their nuclear buildups "like the victims of some sort of hypnotism, like men in a dream, like lemmings heading for the sea. . . ." The technological imperative is fueled by a military-industrial-academic complex that has amassed great political powers.

Convinced that only an informed and caring citizenry can stand in the way of such power to destroy, the Council of Bishops wanted to explore in the light of new and harsh realities a Christian theology of peacemaking. Important policy debates on such crucial issues as deterrence and the Strategic Defense Initiative came in for scrutiny. Relatively unexplored areas of the domestic impact and the social justice implications of the nuclear arms race were investigated.

Many hundreds of persons have contributed to the final draft of the *Foundation Document*. Specialists in academic, church, and governmental centers across the country contributed papers on designated issues. A two-day public hearing in Washington, DC, allowed a panel of bishops to hear twenty-five key witnesses on crucial aspects of the nuclear crisis. Each bishop appointed an advisory panel to contribute to the study. In November 1985, a first draft was made available for public scrutiny, eliciting an extraordinary amount of thoughtful and expert response from across the country.

The Episcopal Initiatives Committee in charge of the project consisted of Bishops C. Dale White, chairperson; C. P. Minnick, Jr., project coordinator; Thomas S. Bangura; Roy C. Clark; W. T. Handy, Jr.; Leroy C. Hodapp; Calvin D. McConnell; and H. Ellis Finger, Jr., assistant to the secretary of the Council of Bishops. Dr. Alan Geyer, Executive Director of the Churches' Center for Theology and Public Policy, was the expert research coordinator, consultant, and principal writer of the document. Holly Wells gave invaluable support as staff assistant. A staff support group assigned by the general secretaries of the major boards and agencies of the church offered essential service. We are especially grateful to Jack Keller and The United Methodist Publishing House and to Bill Richards and Bill Dale of United Methodist Communications for the doors they opened and the resources they prepared.

—Bishop C. Dale White

Foreword

The Council of Bishops of The United Methodist Church, meeting in Orlando, Florida, on November 13, 1984, unanimously approved a report of its Committee on Episcopal Initiatives for Ministry and Mission proposing "a major two-year intervention by the Council of Bishops to mobilize the church to witness and action in the face of the major threat to human survival in our time: the nuclear arms race." The Committee was authorized to prepare a study document and pastoral letter on the nuclear crisis and the pursuit of peace to be used in an intensive program of "study, organization, and action in each Episcopal area or annual conference, in cooperation with the peace and justice programs of the general agencies."

The Council of Bishops adopted the first drafts of this *Foundation Document* and the *Pastoral Letter*, both titled IN DEFENSE OF CREATION: THE NUCLEAR CRISIS AND A JUST PEACE, at the Council's meeting in Wichita, Kansas, November 10-15, 1985. Final drafts were approved at the April 27-May 2, 1986, Council meeting in Morristown, New Jersey. The *Foundation Document* provides the theological, analytical, and practical foundation for the *Pastoral Letter*. It is the product of nearly two years of our own prayerful and penitent study. Four meetings of the Council of Bishops and numerous meetings of the Committee on Episcopal Initiatives have deliberated substantially on the issues. We have invited all the areas, agencies, and institutions of The United Methodist Church to submit views and proposals to us. We are deeply grateful to all who have done so. We held a two-day public hearing in Washington, DC, July 15 and 16, 1985, at which

9

twenty-five witnesses from the government, the military, universities, research institutes, citizen movements, other denominations, and our own churches and seminaries offered both written and oral testimony.

The church of Jesus Christ is blessed with fresh hosts of peacemakers on every continent. We praise the Lord for the historic peace churches whose steadfast witness has been renewed yet again by their 1980 *New Call to Peacemaking*. We bless the Lord for the Presbyterian Church (USA) and its 1980 platform, *Peacemaking: The Believers' Calling*, creating a denominationwide mission that serves as an exemplary model for major Protestant communions. We thank God for the ecumenical testimony of the World Council of Churches, which, especially since its Amsterdam Public Hearing of 1981, has brought the multinational perspectives of Christians on all sides of global conflicts to bear on nuclear weapons and disarmament. We are grateful to God for the US National Conference of Catholic Bishops, whose 1983 pastoral letter, *The Challenge of Peace: God's Promise and Our Response*, provided a remarkably wide and deep study of nuclear issues and of the pastoral challenge they raise.

We seek to renew our own United Methodist heritage, which provides a firm platform for faithful witness to the things that make for peace. That heritage is referred to throughout this document. We make our appeal through all four dimensions of the Wesleyan Quadrilateral: Scripture, tradition, reason, and experience.

We seek the fullest and fairest possible discussion not only of the convictions that we have tried to state clearly but also of alternative and critical views. We pray that our churches may become redemptive models of peaceable diversity even as they struggle for reconciliation and unity in the peace of Christ.

Overview*

We write in defense of creation. We do so because the creation itself is under attack. Air and water, trees and fruits and flowers, birds and fish and cattle, all children and youth, women and men live under the darkening shadows of a threatening nuclear winter. We call The United Methodist Church to more faithful witness and action in the face of this worsening nuclear crisis. It is a crisis that threatens to assault not only the whole human family but planet earth itself, even while the arms race itself cruelly destroys millions of lives in conventional wars, repressive violence, and massive poverty.

We seek the fullest and fairest possible discussion not only of the convictions that we have tried to state clearly but also of alternative and critical views. We pray that our churches may become redemptive models of peaceable diversity even as they struggle for reconciliation and unity in Christ.

The Heritage of Faith and the Call to Peace

The transcendent dimensions of the nuclear crisis make biblical dramas of the human predicament more vivid and more appropriate than most previous generations could know. Too much Christian discussion of war and peace over the intervening centuries has lost the breadth and depth of scriptural understanding of creation, God's action in history,

---

*The Overview serves as both an introduction to and a summary of the entire *Foundation Document*. It is not intended as a substitute for reading the complete argument presented in this document. Some readers may find it most helpful to refer to the Overview again after reading Chapters 1 through 6.   —Editor

the world of nations, and human destiny. Nuclear issues raise questions of freedom and responsibility, the end of history, the meaning of power and security, and spiritual despair. The Bible gives us a faith view and a world view spacious enough to comprehend the enormity of just such issues.

At the heart of Old Testament Scripture is the Hebrew understanding of *shalom*. *Shalom* means positive peace, joyful peace, just peace. *Shalom* is harmony between humanity and all of God's creation. In *shalom* there is no contradiction between justice and peace or between peace and security or between love and justice (Isaiah 32:16-18; Jeremiah 29:7). In the *shalom* of God's good creation, every person of every race in every nation is a sacred being, made in God's image and entitled to life and peace, health and freedom.

But the *shalom* of God's good creation has been broken by the fallenness and violence of sinful human creatures. The powers of government are not only legitimate expressions of the creation's natural order of political community; they are necessary constraints upon human sinfulness. When governments themselves become destroyers of community and threats to the creation, when they presume to usurp the sovereignty that belongs to God alone, they are rightly subject to challenge and correction, protest and resistance. *Shalom* discloses an alternative community—alternative to the idolatries, oppressions, and violence that mark the ways of many nations.

Jesus Christ, the Incarnation of God, comes to us as the presence and promise of *shalom*. He comes heralded by angels who sing: "Glory to God and peace on earth!" He invokes the most special blessings upon peacemakers (Matthew 5:9). He commands us to love our enemies; for he knows, even if we do not, that if we hate our enemies, we blind and destroy ourselves (Matthew 5:43-46; Luke 6:27-38). He weeps when he foresees the city reduced to rubble and dust because the people do not know "the things that make for peace" (Luke 19:41-44).

Paul's letters announce that Jesus Christ is our peace. It is Christ who has "broken down the dividing wall of hostility," creating one new humanity (Ephesians 2:14-19). It is Christ who calls us to become ambassadors of a new creation, a new Kingdom, a new order of love and justice (2 Corinthians 5:17-20). It is Christ who has "disarmed the principalities and powers" (Colossians 2:15). Beyond all brutality and suffering and death, God's costly gift of peace awaits us. Peace is the ultimate victory—peace that the world itself cannot give.

We believe the nuclear crisis poses fundamental questions of faith that neither the pacifist nor just-war traditions have adequately addressed. We invite pacifists and nonpacifists among our people not only to recapture their common ground, such as their moral presumption against all war and violence, but to undertake together a fresh inquiry into those transcendent issues that stretch far beyond private conscience and rational calculation.

The just-war tradition, originating with Saint Ambrose and Saint Augustine in the fourth and fifth centuries, set forth seven principles concerning the morality of going to war and the conduct of warfare. Three of those principles are especially tested by nuclear warfare and have helped us form our own judgments.

First, we are convinced that no actual use of nuclear weapons offers any *reasonable hope of success* in achieving a just peace.

Second, we believe that the principle of *discrimination* (requiring the immunity of noncombatants from direct attack) is bound to be horribly violated in any likely use of nuclear weapons not only because of the widespread effects of blast, fire, radioactive fallout, and environmental damage but also because of the unlikelihood that any resort to nuclear weapons by major powers can result in a strictly controlled or "limited" nuclear war.

Third, we cannot imagine that the norm of *proportionality* can be meaningfully honored in a nuclear war, since such a war could not be waged with any realistic expectation of doing more good than harm.

These considerations impel us to say *No*, a clear and unconditioned *No*, to nuclear war and to any use of nuclear weapons.

But our *No* is more than a matter of ethical calculation; it is a rejection of that nuclear idolatry that presumes to usurp the sovereignty of the God of *shalom* over all nations and peoples. Vengeful judgment and mass destruction are clearly contrary to the will of God and to the moral order of creation.

In the roundedness of *shalom,* a just-war ethic is never enough. Our churches must nurture a *new theology for a just peace.* Our searching of the Scriptures and historical traditions, along with our discernment of the most salient religious issues in the nuclear crisis, has led us to formulate a provisional list of guiding principles for a theology for a just peace. These principles are set forth in Chapter 1 of this document.

The Nuclear Challenge to Faith

Theological understandings of justice and peace in the nuclear crisis must be informed by a distinction between two sets of nuclear issues. There are the *primal issues* of blast, fire, and fallout and their more- or less-direct physical impact. There are also the *consequent issues,* the second- and third-generation issues, which have to do with the many long-term ramifications of all nuclear technologies not only for the physical environment but for all human institutions and behavior: political, economic, scientific, educational, cultural, and psychological. Our churches must give more urgent response to these consequent issues. These are the issues that stretch farthest beyond the classical war-peace debate. They cut most sharply into the fabric of our cultural and institutional life. They make most clear that the nuclear crisis is a matter of *social justice as well as world peace.*

Nuclear deterrence has too long been reverenced as the idol of national security. In its most idolatrous forms it has blinded its proponents to the many-sided requirements of genuine security. There can be no unilateral security in the nuclear age. Security requires economic strength and stability, environmental and public health, educational quality, social well-being, public confidence, and global cooperation.

Whatever claims may be made for deterrence policies since 1945, the future is shadowed by the increasingly perilous trends of recent years. The moral case for deterrence, even as an interim ethic, has been undermined by unrelenting arms escalation. It has been discredited by the invidious discrimination between nuclear-weapon states and those that have renounced nuclear rights under the 1970 Non-Proliferation Treaty. Nuclear deterrence has become a dogmatic license for perpetual hostility between the superpowers and for their rigid resistance to significant measures of disarmament. A still more fundamental flaw is at the very core of nuclear deterrence: a contradiction between inordinate confidence in the rationality of decision makers and the absolute terror of annihilation.

The ideology of deterrence must not receive the churches' blessing, even as a temporary warrant for holding on to nuclear weapons. The lingering possession of such weapons for a strictly limited time requires a different justification: *an ethic of reciprocity* as nuclear-weapon states act together in agreed stages to eliminate their nuclear weapons. Such an ethic is shaped by a realistic vision of *common security* and the escalation of mutual trust rather than mutual terror.

We do not believe that *strategic defenses* offer either an alternative to deterrence or an enhancement of deterrence. We cannot as bishops claim the expertise to assess all the technologies involved. However, moral and political dimensions of this quest for nuclear defenses can and must be made understandable to our church members. Space defenses may well have provocative and dangerous offensive implications. They threaten to become obstacles to new arms-control agreements. They violate the clear intent and spirit of the ABM Treaty of 1972 and risk the demise of that treaty. At estimated costs of up to one trillion dollars, the US Strategic Defense Initiative (SDI) would surely be the most expensive project ever undertaken by any government or any other institution—with enormous economic and social consequences.

We repeat our conviction that the churches must act on the understanding that the nuclear arms race is not simply an antiwar issue. *The nuclear arms race is an issue of social justice.* Justice is offended in the double standard under which some nations presume nuclear weapons for themselves while denying them to others. Justice is outraged in the unending vertical proliferation of nuclear weapons by the superpowers in violation of Article VI of the Non-Proliferation Treaty. Justice is abused in the overwhelming power of nuclear-weapon states to threaten the self-determination, security, and very life of nonaligned and nonbelligerent nations. Justice is forsaken in the squandering of wealth in the arms race while a holocaust of hunger, malnutrition, disease, and violent death is destroying the world's poorest peoples. Justice is defiled by the superpowers' implication in conventional arms races and proxy wars in the Third World, causing much present suffering and threatening escalation into a nuclear war. The possibilities of nuclear terrorism by revolutionary movements are seriously aggravated by such injustices.

The Arms Race and American Society

Christian concern for social justice has both domestic and international dimensions. Every social institution of militarized states has been profoundly affected by the *consequent* issues: the systemic "fallout" of military technologies and policies. In the United States, democratic decision making has been sharply limited by the speed of missiles, the bureaucratic momentum of technology, and the pervasive web of military-industrial-political-scientific interests. Domestic politics has witnessed the demagogic and deceitful exploitation of nuclear fears to silence the voices of reason.

The US military buildup between 1980 and 1985 has cost $1.2 trillion, or more than $20,000 for an average family of four. In fiscal year 1986, military and related spending will amount to more than half of all discretionary spending by Congress. US arms are now being purchased with food stamps, welfare checks, rent subsidies, Medicaid payments, school lunches, and nutrition supplements for poor mothers and their children. Half of the nation's Black children and two fifths of all Hispanic children now live in poverty. The productivity of the American economy has been severely retarded by the disproportionate allocation of scientific and technical personnel and research funds to military purposes. A decline in industrial efficiency has incurred enormous foreign trade deficits and caused the loss of millions of industrial jobs.

The racial dimensions of this struggle over national priorities are increasingly acute. Black teenage unemployment in May 1985 was 40.4 percent and was concentrated in the deteriorating inner core of older cities, where housing, health services, and education are most deficient. Without a sharp new governmental focus on inner city peoples, racial polarization is bound to intensify. Clearly, the demilitarization of America must be accompanied by a powerful new national commitment to equal opportunity for racially disadvantaged peoples.

The "nuclearism" that permeates a whole culture is reflected psychologically in a simultaneous denial of the problem and a sense of helplessness to cope with it. There is a growing fear of "futurelessness" among young people. For young people and for all citizens, the legitimate need for self-respect as a nation must be lifted above the relentless

barrage of aggressive, competititve, and chauvinistic sentiments that assault them not only in political rhetoric but also
in commercial, recreational, and even educational institutions. Peacemaking must be celebrated as a patriotic
commitment.

These domestic burdens of the arms race weigh heavily on
other nations as well. The prospects for political liberalization, economic progress, and social well-being for the peoples
of the Soviet Union are tragically diminished by the enormous
investment of their government in the military sector. The
economic and social development of some of the world's
poorest countries are distorted and constrained by inordinate
arms expenditures and repressive military establishments.

The Arms Race and World Community

Our consciousness of the biblical truth that all the peoples
of earth are one whole human family has been vivified for our
generation as never before by the emergence of both global
threats and global bonds. The nuclear crisis is not primarily a
matter of missiles; it is a crisis of human community. The
US-Soviet conflict is the most serious stumbling block to a
peaceable and survivable world community. The Soviet
Union remains an authoritarian state, obsessed with secrecy,
repressive of most forms of public protest, overbearing and
sometimes brutal in its attempts to dominate states along its
borders. The invasion of Afghanistan is the most recent
example. But millions of Soviet citizens are united in their
national pride, in their passion for peace and security, in their
determination not to be militarily inferior, and in the
sacrifices they have made for economic and technological
progress.

We have come to recognize that anti-Soviet fears, which are
manipulated for political and ideological purposes, are
perhaps the main hindrance on the US side to constructive
arms negotiations. Each government has given the other
abundant cause for grievance since 1917. But the American
and Soviet peoples share a common humanity, a common
aversion to war, a common horror of nuclear weapons, and a
common hope for their economic and social well-being. More
than ninety-five percent of the world's fifty thousand nuclear
weapons are in the arsenals of the United States and Soviet
Union, clearly indicating their mutual responsibility for

reversing the arms race. While each superpower has some statistical advantages, each can totally destroy the other nation and the whole human family—not once, but many times.

As Christians our capacity to address these moral questions is greatly enhanced by our ecumenical bonds with tens of millions of Christian sisters and brothers in the Soviet Union. This endurance of religious faith and practice seven decades after the Bolshevik Revolution is one of the most remarkable spiritual triumphs of modern history.

The new cold war between the United States and Soviet Union extends to every continent. It tends to turn every North-South issue of economic and social justice into an East-West issue of military confrontation. It is a major source of injustice to the world's poorest peoples, whether through squandering of resources, neglect, repression, exploitation, proxy wars, nuclear arrogance, or failure to construct the institutions of multilateral cooperation required for humane development. We implore all United Methodists to testify to their governments that the national aspirations and human rights of Black South Africans, Central Americans, and Filipinos must not be forsaken for "national security" or anti-Soviet policies.

Policies for a Just Peace

The necessity of reconstructing USA-USSR relations is the crux of the nuclear crisis and an imperative of justice and freedom to all earth's peoples. That reconstruction involves developing a regular and systematic pattern of consultation, including an annual summit conference, between the highest political and military leaders of both countries.

We support the following transitional measures *toward a nuclear-free world:*

1. A comprehensive test ban as the first step toward a mutual and verifiable freeze on the testing, production, and deployment of nuclear weapons—and also as an urgent measure to strengthen the Non-Proliferation Treaty.
2. Consolidation of existing bilateral treaties (ABM Treaty of 1972 and SALT II Treaty) and phased but rapid reduction of nuclear arsenals, while calling upon all other nuclear-weapon states to agree to parallel arms reductions, to the

eventual goal of a mutual and verifiable dismantling of all nuclear armaments.

3. Bans on all offensive and defensive space weapons.

4. A no-first-use (of nuclear weapons) agreement, accompanied by withdrawal of all battlefield nuclear weapons from forward defense areas and also by assurances that no conventional force buildups are preconditions of such a policy.

We oppose all major counterforce weapons on both sides (including US MX, Trident, and Pershing II missiles and Soviet SS-18 and SS-19 land-based missiles, Typhoon submarines and missiles, and SS-20 intermediate-range missiles).

We oppose all efforts to achieve nuclear superiority or to promote confidence in "limited nuclear war," and all weapons systems that hold out false hopes of effective defenses against nuclear weapons.

We believe a political climate more conducive to negotiations might well be fostered by independent US or Soviet initiatives, such as a moratorium on nuclear tests, on flight tests of strategic weapons, or on production of fissionable materials for weapons purposes. Such initiatives would be an invitation to reciprocity. They would demonstrate a willingness to risk a small beginning of trust when nations must choose between growing trust and mutual destruction. Reciprocity also means a readiness to respond to the peaceful initiatives of the other side.

We urge renewed commitment to building the institutional foundations of common security, including UN peace-keeping forces, new instruments of mediation and verification, agencies to facilitate economic conversion, and global systems of governance in matters of economic justice, human rights, and environmental conservation.

We propose that the inseparability of peace and justice be made manifest in truly substantial *disarmament funds for development*. Such funds would be devoted to those economic development activities of the United Nations most effectively aimed at the basic human needs of the world's poorest peoples.

We believe the prime alternative to hostility and violence is nurtured in the ways of peacemaking itself. We therefore urge a much stronger commitment to peace research, studies, and training at all levels of education. We encourage special study of nonviolent civilian defense and peacemaking forces.

19

We recognize that both the imperatives of peacemaking and impulses to violence are to be found in all world religions. We therefore urge educational and religious institutions to develop substantial programs of study, dialogue, and action between Christians and other faith communities in the common quest for peace.

The Church as Peacemaker

The church of Jesus Christ, in the power and unity of the Holy Spirit, is called to serve as an alternative community to an alienated and fractured world: a loving and peaceable international company of disciples transcending all governments, races, and ideologies, reaching out to all "enemies," ministering to all the victims of poverty and oppression.

As United Methodists, we have a particular heritage of a "world parish," global ministries, and an enduring witness for peace and world order. John Wesley counted war as the ultimate evidence of humanity's fallen, sinful state. Our Social Principles statement declares: "We believe war is incompatible with the teachings and example of Christ. We therefore reject war as an instrument of national foreign policy and insist that the first moral duty of all nations is to resolve by peaceful means every dispute that arises between or among them." Our commitment to peace has been persistently renewed in such efforts as the Crusade for a New World Order (1943-48), the 1963 establishment of the Church Center for the United Nations, the 1963 study on *The Christian Faith and War in the Nuclear Age,* the Bishops' Call for Peace and the Self-Development of Peoples (1972-76), the 1984 Episcopal Address, and the adoption by the 1984 General Conference of the statement on *Christian Faith and Disarmament.* We gratefully acknowledge the adoption of similar documents by other Methodist bodies around the world.[1]

Peacemaking is a sacred calling of the gospel, blessed by God, making us *evangelists of shalom.* Peacemaking is ultimately a spiritual issue; it compels the conversion of minds and hearts. Prayer is the armor of the spirit that both humbles and empowers us to be instruments of a peace that is not our own to give. Communal prayer renews our spiritual solidarity with Christians who live constantly with the threat of exile or martyrdom. Prayer humanizes our "enemies" and connects us with them in God's one world.

The nurture of spirituality has its first and greatest opportunity in the intimate community of the family. Family life is the potential greenhouse of all peacemaking. We urge every congregation to develop a peacemaking program for families to "choose life" so that they and their children and children's children may live.

An essential task of Christian education is to help the community of faith understand the nature of commitment to the God of *shalom*. Foundational study of the Bible, Christian tradition, and contemporary struggles of the faith constitute the basic curriculum of our churches' education for peacemaking. Our congregations should learn to confront the most controversial, most faith-testing issues of loyalty and conscience in the struggle for justice and peace.

We believe every form of useful work has its own special opportunities for peacemaking. We call upon our people to lift up the ministry of the laity, especially through *vocational guilds,* as a vital strategy for *shalom*. We urge our churches to help scientists, engineers, and other workers involved in defense industries confront questions of conscience; and we encourage the churches to provide a supporting fellowship in whatever vocational choices such persons make.

Pastors and others who serve in church vocations are the primary gatekeepers of our corporate witness to the things that make for peace. Every aspect of pastoral ministry is an opening for peacemaking. We encourage our churches at every level to develop and provide adequate support for full-time ministries of peace education and action.

One of the most important purposes of Christian peacemaking is to equip people for political ministry—the positive exercise of our God-given power in the political arena. We affirm two essential means of fulfilling this purpose: (1) direct and regular personal engagement of our church members with policy makers in foreign and defense policies of their government and (2) personal involvement of church leaders at every level in nurturing political action as an imperative of *shalom*. For citizens of the US, it is especially important to be in touch not only with members of Congress but also with executive agencies and influential opinion leaders outside of government.

Ecumenism—Christian unity in all the fullness of baptism and Eucharist and common life throughout all the earth—is crucial to peacemaking. We call upon United Methodists everywhere to pray regularly for our Christian sisters and brothers in the Soviet Union and in every other land, to study Russian religious life and thought, and to support ecumenical exchanges with churches in the Soviet Union. We especially celebrate the voice that the World Council of Churches gives to the world's poor and most-abused peoples, whose partnership in peacemaking is the plain imperative of the gospel of Jesus Christ.

CHAPTER 1

The Heritage of Faith
and the Call to Peace

For United Methodists today, as for John Wesley two centuries ago, the Bible is the ultimate source of knowledge and authority. In every age and circumstance, in every time of troubles, we look to Holy Scripture for guidance and for power in knowing and doing the will of God. All postbiblical traditions and contemporary theologies need to be assessed in the light of our best understanding of the full range of biblical truth.

Biblical Foundations

To be scripturally faithful in the 1980's is to interpret the Bible in the struggles of our own history and to discern God's action in that history. If the Old and New Testament writers knew nothing of nuclear weapons, they knew much about God's transcending sovereignty over all the nations. They encountered God's judgment and mercy. They foretold the total devastation of cities. They warned about the possible death of all future generations. And they prophesied a new creation of justice and peace.

We believe it is a serious religious error to give extreme emphasis to the historic differences between biblical generations and our own. Such an emphasis can make scriptural imperatives seem irrelevant to the nuclear crisis and the pursuit of peace. It is not for the sake of a narrow biblicism that we urge a rediscovery of what Karl Barth called "the strange new world of the Bible." Our concern is precisely the opposite: Too much Christian discussion of war and peace over the intervening centuries has lost the breadth and depth of scriptural understanding of creation, God's action in history, the world of nations, and human destiny. In particular, nuclear issues raise questions of the defense of earth itself, human freedom and responsibility, the end of history, justice to nonbelligerent and neglected nations, and the very meaning of such political terms as *security*, *power*, and *spiritual despair*. Such topics simply cannot be grasped within the narrow limits of all-too-typical religious arguments between the claims of individual conscience over killing and the rational calculations of justice by rulers. To decide whether or when or how to wage a war assuredly raises important moral questions. Such a decision about war, however, does not construct the foundations of a just and positive peace in a world constantly in peril of annihilation. In fact, the actual use of nuclear weapons would likely deprive the very word *war* of any moral or historical meaning.

Shalom in Creation, Covenant, and Community

At the heart of the Old Testament is the testimony to *shalom*, that marvelous Hebrew word that means peace. But the peace that is *shalom* is not negative or one-dimensional. It is much more than the absence of war. *Shalom* is positive peace: harmony, wholeness, health, and well-being in all human relationships. It is the natural state of humanity as birthed by God. It is harmony between humanity and all of God's good creation. All of creation is interrelated. Every creature, every element, every force of nature participates in the whole of creation. If any person is denied *shalom*, all are thereby diminished.

To speak of the sovereignty of God over all nations and peoples is to testify to this ordering of the whole creation by the goodness and peaceable will of God. It is therefore to discern the inescapable reality of moral law in the universe. The creation is not a realm of chaos or meaninglessness, however much persons or nations may cause anarchy by their own behavior. This cosmic drama of moral struggle among the nations has been a persistent biblical theme in Methodist teaching about the fallenness of sinful human creatures. In testimony to our hearing panel, theologian Paul Ramsey urged us to remember that "no Bible-believing, *Wesley's Standard Sermons*-packing Methodist preacher ever waited for the twentieth century to teach him the obduracy, the unfathomable wickedness, and the dereliction of human hearts." Human sinfulness is, according to Scripture, a warrant for government, law enforcement, and defense against enemies—and also a warning against the iniquity of governors themselves.

Throughout both Testaments, there is a dual attitude toward political authority. The powers of government are legitimate expressions of the creation's natural order of political community among God's children, as well as constraints upon human sinfulness. Their authority is thus from God—at least provisionally. Rulers are ordinarily to be obeyed. Taxes are ordinarily to be paid. But the moral law implanted in creation transcends the laws of any state or empire. When governors themselves become oppressive and lawless, when they presume to usurp the sovereignty that belongs to God alone, they are rightly subject to criticism, to correction, and, ultimately, to resistance.

For love of his own nation and people, Jeremiah speaks boldly against his kings for their false gods, religious pride, militaristic adventures, and forced labor to build luxurious palaces. For that he is seized by priests, called a traitor, beaten, jailed, and thrown into a slimy cistern. Through such faithful prophets, we know that patriotism is not only to be found on a battlefield against the enemies of one's nation but can also be courageously expressed in a struggle of resistance against the inhumanities of one's own government. Jeremiah foreshadows another prophet, a prophet of a new covenant, who, six centuries later, for the love of his people, would warn his followers that they too would be dragged before governing authorities, even as he would be—a prophet who would be beaten and nailed to a cross.

The Old Testament speaks of God's sovereignty in terms of *covenant*, more particularly the "covenant of peace" with Israel, which binds that people to God's *shalom* (Isaiah 54:10; Ezekiel 37:26). In the covenant of *shalom*, there is no contradiction between justice and peace or between peace and security or between love and justice (Jeremiah 29:7). In Isaiah's prophecy, when "the Spirit is poured upon us from on high," we will know that these laws of God are one and indivisible:

Then justice will dwell in the wilderness,
    and righteousness abide in the fruitful field.
And the effect of righteousness will be peace,

and the result of righteousness, quietness and trust
for ever.
My people will abide in a peaceful habitation,
in secure dwellings, and in quiet resting places.
(Isaiah 32:16-18)

Shalom, then, is the sum total of moral and spiritual
qualities in a community whose life is in harmony with God's
good creation. It indicates an alternative community—alternative to the idolatries, oppressions, and violence that mark
the ways of many nations. Israel's mission is to live out that
alternative pattern of life in the world.

When the rulers fulfill the covenant of *shalom,* they will
know that there is no true security without peace and no true
peace without justice. When, on the contrary, they seek
unjustly to enhance their own security and tell lies to justify
their military ambitions, they will bring down violence and
devastation instead of security or peace:

You have plowed iniquity,
you have reaped injustice,
you have eaten the fruit of lies.
Because you have trusted in your chariots
and in the multitude of your warriors,
therefore the tumult of war shall arise among your
people,
and all your fortresses shall be destroyed.
(Hosea 10:13-14)

The sovereignty of God means that vengeance in human
hands is evil. When in the Song of Moses Yahweh proclaims
"vengeance is mine," the message is not that God is violent
but rather that the people of God have no right to usurp God's
powers of ultimate judgment (Deuteronomy 32:35). We
believe that particular biblical truth is directly relevant to
ethical attitudes toward nuclear weapons.

To be sure, the Old Testament tells of much violence and
warfare. In Israel's earliest traditions Yahweh is often
portrayed as a warrior. God's victory over Pharaoh and the
Egyptians to liberate Hebrew slaves discloses God's implac-
able opposition to oppression and injustice, which violate
shalom. Exodus is liberation.

But liberation from oppression is hardly on the same moral

plane as the building up of standing armies for nationalistic expansion and the oppression of weaker nations. It is when the elders of Israel forsake their moral covenant for warrior-kings that the nation begins its dismal descent into generations of exploitation, repression, and aggression—and then into chaos and captivity. Yahweh, the Creator, the Sovereign One, the transcendent God of the Covenant, becomes reduced to a domesticated and nationalistic idol. Ultimately, as Jeremiah has foreseen, destruction and exile come upon Jerusalem precisely as God's judgment upon nationalistic pride, religious arrogance, and excessive confidence in military power. Exile in Babylon is more than the loss of a war; it is the collapse of an illusion that military power, unrestrained by *shalom*, can offer security, peace, and prosperity.

We must look to the great prophets of that bitter period of Exile for the renewed vision of *shalom*. If Exodus is liberation, Exile is renewal. Ezekiel and Isaiah (40–66) reaffirm God's creation and redemption as universal in scope. Narrow nationalism is repudiated. Servanthood is exalted as the hopeful path to *shalom*.

Swords into plowshares, arms converted to food and death to life, no more wars or training for wars, peaceable kingdoms, joy and peace such that the trees clap their hands, new covenants written on the heart—these are the radiant images of *shalom* at the visionary heights of Old Testament prophecy. With these images we know that the Bible is really one Book. The images forecast the coming of One who will be the Prince of Peace.

Jesus Christ Is Our Peace

And so he comes. He comes heralded by angels who sing: "Glory to God in the highest, and on earth peace!" He invokes the most special blessings upon peacemakers. He exalts the humanity of aliens. He commands us to love our enemies; for he knows, even if we do not, that if we hate our enemies, we blind and destroy ourselves. *Shalom,* after all, is the heart of God and the law of creation. It cannot be broken with impunity.

There is a stark and sorrowful moment when Jesus, approaching Jerusalem from the neighboring heights, pauses to weep. And why does he weep? He foresees a terrible Day of Judgment when the Holy City itself will be totally leveled to rubble and dust without "one stone upon another." Why? Because the people there, even the most religious people in that supposedly sacred city, do not really know "the things that make for peace" (Luke 19:41-44). That moment is a powerful intimation of what false security policies based upon weapons of mass destruction can lead to. It is a poignant echo of Isaiah's lament from the Lord, the Redeemer, the Holy One of Israel:

> O that you had hearkened to my commandments!
> Then your peace would have been like a river,
> and your righteousness like the waves of the sea.
> (Isaiah 48:18)

New Testament faith presupposes a radical break between the follies of much so-called conventional wisdom about power and security, on the one hand, and the transcendent wisdom of *shalom*, on the other. Ultimately, New Testament faith is a message of hope about God's plan and purpose for human destiny. It is a redemptive vision that refuses to wallow in doom. The author of the Epistle of James, which has been called "that secret little apocalypse," testifies to the power of this transcendent wisdom:

> . . . the wisdom from above is first pure, then peaceable, gentle, open to reason, full of mercy and good fruits, without uncertainty or insincerity. And the harvest of righteousness is sown in peace by those who make peace.
> (James 3:17-18)

It is just after these verses that James asks: "What causes wars?" There follows a catalogue of human sins: excess passion, covetousness, pride, arrogance, evil judgments against brothers and neighbors.

Paul's letters announce that Jesus Christ is "our peace." It is Christ who has "broken down the dividing wall of hostility," creating one humanity, overcoming enmity, so making peace (Ephesians 2:14-19). It is Christ who ordains a ministry of reconciliation. Repentance prepares us for reconciliation. Then we shall open ourselves to the transforming power of God's grace in Christ. Then we shall know what it means to be "in Christ." Then we are to become ambassadors of a new creation, a new Kingdom, a new order of love and justice

(2 Corinthians 5:17-20). It is Christ who has "disarmed the principalities and powers and made a public example of them, triumphing over them in him" (Colossians 2:15). To be citizens of this new Kingdom means that Christians are subject to conflicting loyalties—loyalty to one's nation and its government and a transcending loyalty to the "Governor of the whole universe" (John Wesley's term), whose laws may compel us to challenge our nation and its policies.

In Jesus Christ we know, when confronted with such conflicting loyalties, how costly the grace of God can be. This "only begotten Son" is sacrificed in a controversy with imperial and religious authorities so that we may know the full measure of God's love for us, even in our sinfulness, even when we crucify the Christ in our brothers and sisters. Yet we may still come to know that life never really ends but is transformed by eternal grace. Jesus never resorted to violence in his own defense. Somehow he had the power to forgive even his own killers. The Crucifixion is an eternal testimony to the transcendent power of forgiving love and nonviolence.

The Crucifixion was initially a political event—and a seeming defeat at that—but it quickly became transformed into a theological event, the ultimate act of our redemption. Christ is forever "making peace by the blood of his cross" (Colossians 1:19-20). Beyond all brutality, suffering, and death, God's costly gift of peace awaits us. Peace is the ultimate victory. The Catholic bishops' pastoral letter on war and peace declares:

> The resurrection of Jesus is the sign to the world that God indeed does reign, does give life in death, and that the love of God is stronger even than death (Romans 8:36-39).
> Only in light of this . . . can Jesus' gift of peace—a peace that the world cannot give (John 14:27)—be understood. Jesus gives that peace to his disciples, to those who had witnessed the helplessness of the crucifixion and the power of the resurrection (John 20:19, 20, 26). The peace which he gives to them as he greets them as their risen Lord is the fullness of salvation. It is the reconciliation of the world and God (Romans 5:1-2; Colossians 1:20); the restoration of the unity and harmony of all creation which the Old Testament spoke of with such longing.[2]

The promise of peace envisioned by Israel's prophets of the Exile at the climax of the Old Testament is celebrated once more at the climax of the New Testament. The Revelation of John, in the darkest night of despair, sings of a new earth, radiant with infinite love and compassion, in which all nations and peoples come together peaceably before the Lord God and in which hunger and hurt and sorrow are no more (Revelation 7).

The Diversity of Traditions

Despite the biblical heritage of *shalom,* there has been a conspicuous lack of harmony among Christians, especially since the fourth century, concerning the ethics of war and peace. Disharmonies have not simply represented the varied opinions of biblical scholars and theologians; they have reflected national, cultural, and class perceptions and prejudices. They have been expressed in public controversy and civil strife, even to the repression and persecution of Christian dissenters. They have been most horribly invoked in murderous crusades and bloody Wars of Religion.

Over the centuries three classical positions developed among Christian thinkers and church bodies: pacifism, "just-war" doctrine, and the crusade. While this threefold division never fully reflected the diversity of Christian views, it is particularly outmoded and inadequate for clarifying the ethical dilemmas of the nuclear arms race. Nevertheless, proponents of those classical positions have seriously addressed these dilemmas. Here we sketch the three traditions in briefest outline before addressing the central nuclear issues and proposing a new and more varied ethical spectrum.

The Pacifist Tradition

The early church of the first four centuries was predominantly pacifist. For most Christians, being pacifist meant opposition to all killing, military service, and warfare. Their scriptural seriousness and their historical proximity to Jesus and his immediate followers have remained a persuasive warrant for the pacifist witness ever since.

Justin Martyr (about A.D. 100-165) announced that Jesus Christ was the fulfillment of Isaiah's promise of peace. Christians, therefore, have "in every part of the world converted our weapons of war into implements of peace—our swords into plowshares, our spears into farmers' tools . . . ."[3] This unwillingness of Christians to fight in the military campaigns of the Roman Empire evoked a severe scolding in A.D. 178 from Celsus, a pagan critic: "If everyone were to do the same as you, there would be nothing to prevent [the king] from being abandoned, alone and deserted, while earthly things would come into the power of the most lawless and savage barbarians . . . ."[4]

There were surely other reasons for this early pacifism, reasons such as rejection of the idolatry of emperor-worship, which was required in the military oath of allegiance; the generally sectarian, nonpolitical orientation of church life within the empire; and an apocalyptic expectation of the end of the world.

However, the pacifist tradition outlived the Roman Empire and the Constantinian establishment of Christianity in the fourth century. At the summit of medieval sainthood and spirituality stood Francis of Assisi, whose winsome embodiment of the *shalom* of all creation and whose prayers for peace remain a special inspiration to peacemakers of every generation. Renaissance Christianity, three centuries after Francis, was graced with the pacifist testimony of the brilliant Erasmus of Rotterdam (1466-1536). His tract, *The Complaint of Peace*, marveled at the peaceableness of subhuman creatures among their own kind, in contrast to the warring tendencies of humans, even Christians. Among Erasmus's recommendations were procedures for peaceful arbitration and clergy abstention from military rituals.

The Protestant Reformation, like the fifteen preceding centuries, bequeathed a mixed legacy concerning peacemaking. Though neither Luther nor Calvin nor Zwingli could be called pacifist, the Reformation eventually generated several new religious communities that have come to be known collectively as the "historic peace churches" because of their pacifist founders and credos. Among them are the Mennonites, the Church of the Brethren, and the Society of Friends (Quakers).

While John Wesley's attitudes toward the American Revolution were ambivalent (he was a man of Tory sentiments), his essay on "The Doctrine of Original Sin" focused on war as the prime example of human depravity. Many of the most prominent United Methodist leaders of the twentieth century have been pacifists.

Pacifism in this century has received powerful reinforcement from nonwhite, non-Western, and non-Christian sources. While not exclusively identified with pacifism, the nonviolent philosophies of Mahatma Gandhi, Toyohiko Kagawa, Martin Luther King, Jr., Albert Luthuli, and Desmond Tutu have helped make pacifism more credible to our generation. Nonviolent strategies of social change, civilian defense, and conflict resolution have become increasingly sophisticated and systematic, inviting the most serious attention from academic, governmental, and religious leaders. We shall have more to say about the churches' own ministries of peace education and nonviolent action in Chapters 5 and 6.

The Just-War Tradition

The courage and endurance of the pacifist tradition have not prevented most Christians and virtually all governments from appealing to nonpacifist principles in support of military establishments and the resort to war. For many Christians the principle that matters most has been obedience to whatever their government commands. Theological ethicist Stanley Hauerwas, in testimony before our hearing panel, called this tendency the "blank-check" option, as distinct from the conscientious scruples of both pacifist and just-war traditions.

We believe it is a serious mistake to identify just-war doctrine with the "blank-check" option. It is surely true that just-war principles (and even pacifist language) have all too frequently rationalized unjust wars and brutal policies. We are also persuaded that just-war morality provides too narrow a base from which to discern many of the most salient issues in the nuclear crisis.

We cannot agree, however, with those who claim that nuclear weapons have simply nullified the just-war tradition altogether. That tradition remains a morally earnest restraint on the resort to war, a summons to peaceful settlement, and a guide to humane conduct in the event of war. Just-war criteria provided many young nonpacifist Americans with an ethical basis for challenging US policies in Indochina and for formulating a position of selective conscientious objection, which has been repeatedly validated in United Methodist pronouncements. The 1976 General Conference declared its support for "all those who conscientiously object to preparation for or participation in any specific war or all wars; . . . and we ask that they be granted legal recognition."

The US Catholic bishops, while modestly acknowledging the inadequacy of their own traditional teachings, helpfully restated just-war principles as the foundation for their critique of nuclear warfare and weapons in their 1983 pastoral letter, as did the 1982 General Convention of the Episcopal Church in adopting the report of its Joint Commission on Peace. However, while Roman Catholic and Episcopal documents finally appeal to just-war arguments to support nuclear deterrence, we are persuaded that the logic of this tradition ultimately discredits nuclear deterrence as a morally tenable position. We would welcome a continuing ecumenical discussion of this issue.

We seek to keep the just-war tradition alive, even as we seek to keep the pacifist tradition alive, each serving as a partial but vital testimony to the requirements of justice and peace. Both pacifist and just-war traditions profess integrity between the ends and the means of action.

The principal criteria of the just-war tradition evolved over many centuries, beginning with Saint Ambrose and Saint Augustine in the fourth and fifth centuries, and were elaborated by Saint Thomas Aquinas and other moral philosophers in the medieval and modern periods. A distinction was made between principles concerning the *just resort to war (jus ad bellum)* and those concerning *just conduct in war (jus in bello)*.

The five most common *jus ad bellum* principles are:

(1) **Just cause**. A decision for war must vindicate justice itself in response to some serious evil, such as an aggressive attack.

(2) **Just intent**. The ends sought in a decision for war must include the restoration of peace with justice and must not seek self-aggrandizement or the total devastation of another nation.

(3) **Last resort**. This tradition shares with pacifism a moral presumption against going to war—but is prepared to make exceptions. Every possibility of peaceful settlement of a conflict must be tried before war is begun.

(4) **Legitimate authority**. A decision for war may be made and declared only by properly constituted governmental authority.

(5) **Reasonable hope of success**. A decision for war must be based on a prudent expectation that the ends sought can

be achieved. It is hardly an act of justice to plunge one's people into the suffering and sacrifice of a suicidal conflict.

The two main *jus in bello* principles are:

(6) **Discrimination**. Justice in the actual conduct of war requires respect for the rights of enemy peoples, especially for the immunity of noncombatants from direct attack. Such respect also rules out atrocities, reprisals, looting, and wanton violence.

(7) **Proportionality**. The amount of damage inflicted must be strictly proportionate to the ends sought. Small-scale injuries should not be avenged by massive suffering, death, and devastation. The war's harm must not exceed the war's good. (Proportionality is also a criterion to be applied to *jus ad bellum*—the decision whether to resort to war in the first place.)

These just-war principles remain morally stringent in our time. Three of these principles are especially tested by nuclear warfare.

First, we are convinced that no actual use of nuclear weapons offers any *reasonable hope of success* in achieving a just peace. Whether the "mere" possession of such weapons, with an explicit or implicit threat to use them, is morally justifiable again raises the topic of deterrence, which we shall be discussing in Chapter 2.

Second, we believe that the principle of *discrimination,* whatever the intention of political and military leaders, is bound to be horribly violated in any likely use of nuclear weapons not only because of the widespread effects of blast, fire, fallout, and environmental damage but also because of the unlikelihood that any resort to nuclear weapons by major powers can result in a strictly controlled or "limited" nuclear war. The consequences are likely to be global.

Third, we cannot imagine that the norm of *proportionality* can be meaningfully honored in a nuclear war, since such a war could not be waged with any realistic expectation of doing more good than harm.

These considerations posed by the still-valuable just-war tradition require us to say *No*, a clear and unconditioned *No*, to nuclear war and to any use of nuclear weapons.

But our *No* to nuclear war and weapons is more than a matter of ethical calculation. It is a refusal to participate in that nuclear idolatry that presumes to usurp the sovereignty of the

God of *shalom* over all the nations and peoples. Vengeful judgment and mass destruction are clearly contrary to the will of God and to the moral order of creation.

Other significant nuclear issues are not directly addressed by either pacifist or just-war principles, even though they too are issues of justice, as we shall see.

In the roundedness of *shalom,* a just-war ethic is never enough. Our churches must nurture a *new theology for a just peace.*

The Crusade Tradition

The fusion of political and religious authority in the Middle Ages fostered a third Christian tradition in matters of war and peace: crusades against infidels. The capture of Jerusalem's holy places by the Turks at the end of the eleventh century was cited to make warfare itself a holy cause and even a path to sainthood.

Unlike the pacifist and just-war traditions, which share a moral presumption against war, the crusade assumes that an unrestrained conduct of war is a religious obligation. A holy war need not stop to count the casualties on either side; "higher" values are at stake. The sixteenth century's Wars of Religion turned the crusade tradition inward and produced Christian massacres by fellow Christians.

If the crusade tradition seems today like a quaint relic of past centuries, we forget the excess of self-righteousness and the barbarism with which almost all modern wars have been waged. Moral restraints have been overwhelmed; and poison gas, fire raids, nuclear weapons, and napalm have been used. In the 1980's some religious groups promote a nuclear arms buildup and a militantly anti-Soviet foreign policy, with a heavy accent on "atheistic communism" as the enemy of the faith.

It is the advent of a new cold war in the 1980's and the regression of USA-USSR relations to the worst period of ideological animosities that provides much of the political context for the nuclear crisis we seek to overcome. We hope that the recent resumption of summit diplomacy between US and Soviet leaders will soon lead to decisive measures of nuclear disarmament. We do not doubt that there are morally significant differences among the world's political, social, and economic systems. That is the lingering kernel of truth in the crusade tradition. But we cannot imagine that any such differences will ever justify the waging of a nuclear war.

35

A Theology for a Just Peace: Guiding Principles

Our searching of the Scriptures and historical traditions, along with our discernment of the most salient religious issues of the nuclear crisis, has led us to formulate a provisional list of guiding principles for a theology for a just peace. We invite reflection, amendment, and enrichment.

1. Perfect peace is beyond human power; it is that grace that is the whole of God's love in action. For Christians, that grace is ultimately the gift of God through Jesus Christ.

2. Every person of every race in every nation is a sacred being, made in God's image, entitled to full participation in the *shalom* of God's good creation—to life and peace, health and freedom.

3. Peacemaking is a sacred calling of the gospel, especially blessed by God, making us evangelists of *shalom*—peace that is overflowing with justice, compassion, and well-being.

4. God's gift of genuine freedom to humanity includes the possibility of humanity's self-destruction.

5. Peacemaking in the nuclear age, under the sovereignty of God, requires the defense of creation itself against possible assaults that may be rationalized in the name of "national defense."

6. Government is a natural institution of human community in God's creation as well as a requirement for the restraint of human evil.

7. Every policy of government must be an act of justice and must be measured by its impact on the poor, the weak, and the oppressed—not only in our own nation but in all nations.

8. Loyalty to one's own government is always subject to the transcendent loyalty that belongs to the Sovereign God alone. Such loyalty may be politically expressed either in support of or in opposition to current government policies.

9. Security is not only a legitimate concern but also an imperative responsibility of governments for the protection of life and well-being. But the security of which biblical prophets speak cannot be separated from the moral imperatives of justice and peace and the full range of basic human needs.

10. Security is indivisible in a world threatened with total

annihilation. Unilateral security is impossible in the nuclear age.

11. The transformation of our conflict-ridden nation-state system into a new world order of common security and interdependent institutions offers the only practical hope for enduring peace.

12. No nation may presume the powers of ultimate judgment on the fate of other nations, even to their destruction.

13. The Gospel command to love enemies is more than a benevolent ideal; it is essential to our own well-being and even to our survival.

14. Repentance is a prerequisite of reconciliation for individuals, groups, nations, and churches. The churches' own implication in militarism, racism, sexism, and materialism requires a deeply penitent approach to peacemaking.

15. Truthfulness is a necessary foundation of peacemaking. Lies tend to become tools of self-aggrandizement, weapons of hate, and acts of violence.

16. All Christians, pacifists and nonpacifists alike, ought to share a strong moral presumption against violence, killing, and warfare, seeking every possible means of peaceful conflict resolution.

17. Any just resort to coercive force must seek the restoration of peace with justice, refrain from directly attacking noncombatants, and avoid causing more harm than good.

18. No just cause can warrant the waging of nuclear war or any use of nuclear weapons.

19. The church of Jesus Christ, in the power and unity of the Holy Spirit, is called to serve as an alternative community to an alienated and fractured world—a loving and peaceable international company of disciples transcending all governments, races, and ideologies; reaching out to all "enemies"; and ministering to all the victims of poverty and oppression.

20. Ecumenism, in all the fullness of baptism and Eucharist, and in common life throughout all the earth, is the new synonym for peacemaking.

CHAPTER 2

The Nuclear Challenge
to Faith

In the decades since Hiroshima, the theological and ethical questions have become more complex than the fact of the Bomb itself. Problematical developments include:

- [ ] The persistence of cold war animosities and rivalries.
- [ ] The hazards of nuclear testing.
- [ ] The elaboration of strategic nuclear doctrines in the name of "national security."
- [ ] An uncontrolled arms race producing more than fifty thousand nuclear weapons.
- [ ] Arms costs in the trillions of dollars in the face of massive world poverty and hunger.
- [ ] The political ascendancy of military-industrial complexes in all nuclear-weapon states.
- [ ] The quickening of military technology not only in explosives but also in missiles, electronics, computers, lasers, and many other fields.
- [ ] New dilemmas of governmental authority, including command, communications, and control, with regard to decisions about the use of nuclear weapons.
- [ ] Nuclear energy systems with problems of safety, security, waste disposal, and unanticipated costs.
- [ ] The actual and potential proliferation of nuclear weapons to other countries and terrorist movements.
- [ ] Possible ozone depletion, exposing earthlings to increasingly lethal ultraviolet rays from the sun.
- [ ] Nuclear-winter studies forecasting earth-threatening layers of dust and smoke.
- [ ] A new psychological literature about "nuclear numbing" and "futurelessness."

In view of these manifold developments since Hiroshima, all deserving of serious religious and ethical response, we find it necessary to distinguish between two rather different sets of nuclear issues. While these sets are somewhat overlapping, they tend to provide radically different agendas for the nuclear debate.

First, there are the *primal issues* of blast, fire, and fallout—the hard reality of nuclear weapons themselves, their more- or less-direct physical impact, and the moral questions as to whether or how to make or use them.

There are also the *consequent issues* having to do with all those problematical developments since 1945, mentioned above. These are "second- and third-generation issues" concerning the many long-term ramifications of nuclear technologies not only for the physical environment but also for all human institutions and behavior: political, economic, scientific, educational, cultural, and psychological. While the world has so far been spared any further nuclear warfare, there has been a widespread assault on humane values.

We confess that the churches' response to *primal* nuclear issues over the past four decades has been fitful and feeble. At the same time, we recognize that some theologians in the first years after Hiroshima, and again in the 1980's, have earnestly sought to address these primal issues. Typically, they have drawn on pacifist and just-war traditions in their efforts.

We are equally troubled by the inadequate response of churches and theologians to the *consequent* nuclear issues. These consequent issues stretch farthest beyond the classical war-peace debate. They cut most sharply into the systemic fabric of our cultural and institutional life. They make most clear that the nuclear crisis is an issue of *social justice* as well as world peace. And they make the wholeness of the *shalom* vision most imperative for our time.

The Ethical Spectrum on Nuclear Weapons

As most denominations and ecumenical bodies have become freshly engaged in the nuclear debate since 1980, the classical threefold typology (pacifist/just-war/crusade) has proved increasingly inadequate to contain the burgeoning variety of ethical positions. The sevenfold spectrum we offer here is largely concerned with what we have called the *primal issues*: the elemental questions as to whether any possession or use of nuclear weapons is morally permissible.

Inevitably, such a spectrum emphasizes differing views concerning the dominant US strategic doctrine since 1945—*nuclear deterrence*. Simply defined, deterrence is the threat to retaliate. Secretary of Defense Caspar Weinberger, in a 1985 statement forwarded to our hearing panel, asserted: "The keystone of our military strategy since World War II has been deterrence. Deterrence provides security by convincing potential adversaries that the risks and costs of aggression will exceed any conceivable gains."[5]

As a war prevention strategy, deterrence represents a just cause. As a potential holocaust, deterrence represents unimaginable evil. Christian thinkers differ greatly in their attitudes toward this awesome moral ambiguity.

Traditional Pacifism

Those who conscientiously repudiate all warfare and weapons of war have a clear answer to the question of nuclear weapons: No—no production, no possession, no deployment, no use. From this perspective, nuclear deterrence is illegitimate and immoral because it rationalizes the possession, if not the use, of the weapons themselves.

We believe the fidelity and endurance of this tradition among a sizable minority of Christians point to a fundamental question of the nuclear age: Can any major war remain non-nuclear? If not, hasn't rejection of war itself become an imperative for all our churches?

Our own United Methodist Church, while never claiming to be one of the historic peace churches or officially pacifist, has adopted by General Conference action a statement of Social Principles that declares:

We believe war is incompatible with the teachings and example of Christ. We therefore reject war as an instrument of national foreign policy and insist that the first moral duty of all nations is to resolve by peaceful means every dispute that arises between or among them; that human values must outweigh military claims as governments determine their priorities; that the militarization of society must be challenged and stopped; that the manufacture, sale, and deployment of armaments must be reduced and controlled; and that the production, possession, or use of nuclear weapons be condemned.

Nuclear Pacifism

Some Christians support conventional military forces and remain open to the possible justice or necessary evil of some wars or revolutions but say No to all nuclear wars and weapons. For them the "nuclear threshold" is an absolute moral boundary that must never be crossed. They may appeal to the historic prerequisites of a "just war" in Christian tradition, such as proportionality and civilian immunity, in judging that nuclear weapons are too destructive ever to serve the ends of justice. Or, oppositely, they may come to the conviction that the just-war tradition itself has been made obsolete by the enormity of any nuclear conflict.

A position of virtual nuclear pacifism (although that term was not used) was set forth by the World Council of Churches Sixth Assembly in Vancouver in 1983:

> We believe that the time has come when the churches must unequivocally declare that the production and deployment as well as the use of nuclear weapons are a crime against humanity and that such activities must be condemned on ethical and theological grounds.[6]

In that same "Statement on Peace and Justice," the Assembly rejected the doctrine of nuclear deterrence as "morally unacceptable and as incapable of safeguarding peace and security in the long-term."[7]

Yes/No Deterrence

While nuclear pacifists draw the moral line between conventional and nuclear weapons, others draw the line between *possession* of nuclear weapons and their actual *use*. They say Yes to having them but No to using them. They are prepared to maintain a nuclear arsenal for its presumed deterrent effect but they have absolute scruples against using the weapons.

Among Christian theologians confessing to such an ambiguous stance have been John C. Bennett, former president of New York's Union Theological Seminary, and David Hollenbach, Jesuit professor at Weston Seminary. Father Hollenbach's recent book, *Nuclear Ethics*, pleads for a new synthesis of pacifist and just-war thinking. He candidly acknowledges the apparent inconsistency in his position:

> It would be easy to conclude that deterrence and the rejection of use are incompatible were it not for a single, massive historical fact: large numbers of nuclear weapons are already deployed and ready for use by both superpowers. Though incompatible on the level of ideas and logic, deterrence and non-use are concretely and existentially interlocked in our present world. This . . . is a prime example of what it means to live in a world which is not fully rational and which is broken by sinfulness.[8]

Critics of this position have dubbed it "bluff deterrence" (or even "clergy deterrence") because its proponents are not really prepared to retaliate. The credibility of yes/no deterrence is therefore a vexing question.

No First Use/Deterrence

Another moral boundary is drawn by those who approve of the possession and possible use of nuclear weapons, but absolutely oppose any use of them against a conventional attack. This restriction of nuclear retaliation to only a nuclear attack is termed a "no-first-use" policy.

Such a policy has yet to be adopted by the US government. However, it was strongly recommended in 1982 by four eminent former officials: McGeorge Bundy (National Security Adviser), George F. Kennan (Ambassador to the Soviet Union), Robert S. McNamara (Secretary of Defense), and Gerard Smith (Director of the Arms Control and Disarmament Agency). Their advocacy of a "no-first-use" policy in a *Foreign Affairs* article raised the question as to whether NATO's conventional forces might need strengthening as a precondition of such a policy change.[9] That article clearly was taken seriously by the US Catholic bishops, who endorsed "no first use" and also "reluctantly" raised the prospect of "some strengthening of conventional defense." They proposed "rigid restrictions" on deployment of nuclear weapons in Europe, according to the *jus in bello* norms of the just-war tradition: discrimination and proportionality.

On the occasion of the Second United Nations Special Session on Disarmament in June 1982, Pope John Paul II (represented by Vatican Secretary of State Cardinal Casaroli) offered an extraordinary moral justification for nuclear weapons:

> In current conditions "deterrence" based on balance, certainly not as an end in itself but as a step on the way toward a progressive disarmament, may still be judged morally acceptable. Nonetheless in order to ensure peace, it is indispensable not to be satisfied with this minimum which is always susceptible to the real danger of explosion.[10]

This crucial passage quoted in the Catholic Pastoral is now at the center of ecumenical debate on nuclear weapons. A passage in an earlier draft that had listed five "negative dimensions of deterrence" was eliminated in the final draft.

First Use/Deterrence

A still lower nuclear threshold is advocated by those who want to preserve the option of nuclear retaliation against conventional attack. This has been a major element in US and NATO policy since the early 1960's. That policy has tended to assume the possibility of a limited nuclear war—limited targeting, limited destruction, and the essential survival of belligerent nations.

The mainstream of official US deterrence doctrine for many years has tended to assume not only the continued deployment of nuclear weapons into the far future but also the continuation of the arms race itself and the prospect of limited nuclear wars. Arms control, from this perspective, means "managing" the arms race so that a nuclear balance is maintained between the superpowers. Parity is the norm that matters. The title of a recent Harvard study, *Living With Nuclear Weapons,* suggests this position's skepticism about nuclear disarmament.[11]

This position also finds plausible support in the *jus in bello* norms of proportionality and discrimination as guides for the actual use of nuclear weapons. Thus a Christian case has been made for *counterforce* strategies—restricting the targeting of nuclear weapons to military forces and command centers while sparing civilian populations. Paul Ramsey has long been the most notable exponent of such a case, emphasizing that nuclear weapons cannot now be uninvented; that the moral boundary between nuclear and conventional weapons is not absolute; that "economy of force" should guide the design and possible use of nuclear weapons; and that Christians should be open to the support of new counterforce weapons like the single-warhead "Midgetman," which might be a move away from more-massive yet more-vulnerable strategic weapons such as a ten-warhead MX missile.

Current US "modernization" of strategic weapons, especially with improved precision guidance systems, is justified by such counterforce doctrine and is heralded as a moral advance beyond "mutual assured destruction" (M.A.D.).

We must now call attention to a disturbing fact: These sharply contrasting moral views on nuclear weapons, from nuclear pacifism to moderate deterrence to limited nuclear war and infinite escalation, all appeal to just-war doctrine to support their case. There is no consensus on the application of the just-war tradition to nuclear weapons.

Similarly, we are concerned that the doctrine of nuclear deterrence itself, which some churches justify by the just-war tradition, can be invoked for the most varied moral postures—from mere possession of nuclear weapons to their limited or even total use and now, as we shall see, to nuclear superiority and even the hope of victory in a nuclear war. We find no coherence in deterrence.

Counterforce Superiority

While counterforce principles may seek to restrain the destructiveness of nuclear weapons, they may also rationalize opposite tendencies: making the use of such weapons more "thinkable" and building up more-powerful and more-accurate weapons to achieve nuclear superiority. For some Americans, parity with the Soviet Union isn't good enough. Only when the United States can prove its capacity to outstrip the Soviet Union in the arms race will the Soviet Union begin seriously to negotiate arms control and accommodate to the demands of the United States on other issues—or so this position maintains.

In the early 1980's there was talk in high places in the US of achieving a nuclear "war-winning capability." In the face of public criticism, Secretary of Defense Caspar Weinberger in 1983 denied that the US really planned to "win" a nuclear war. The goal was rather to "prevail" in such a war. In 1984 President Reagan moderated his own language to declare that "a nuclear war cannot be won and must never be fought."

We have not been able to discern the difference between

"winning" and "prevailing." On occasion, the same policies are propounded with the modest claim that the United States is only trying to restore a balance, which the Soviet Union is alleged to have upset by its own drive for superiority. At times official proponents of counterforce superiority characterize their position as one of "enhancing deterrence." The new counterforce threat, however, goes beyond retaliation against attack. Its very technologies are designed to destroy the adversary's own retaliatory forces—to have "hard-target kill capability," in official jargon. Such weapons tend to destroy confidence in whatever stability there may seem to be in mutual deterrence. Some official counterforce strategists, however, claim that deterrence itself is inadequate, or immoral, or soon to be obsolete. Counterforce is thus justified as a critical alternative to deterrence. Once again we are concerned, and we ask all our members to be concerned, about the apparent lack of coherent and consistent guidance of US nuclear weapons policy.

First-Strike Policies

Both the United States and Soviet Union now officially disavow any intention of preparing for a first strike—initiating an all-out nuclear attack that would destroy the other side's strategic nuclear forces and much else besides. In his *Annual Report to the Congress, Fiscal Year 1986,* Secretary of Defense Weinberger claimed: "We do not have, nor do we seek, a first-strike capability; we do not have a 'nuclear warfighting' posture; all of our exercises and doctrines are defensive in nature."[12]

But the Secretary of Defense went on to charge the USSR with "development of a potential first-strike force of SS-18s and SS-19s" (heavy land-based missiles). Meanwhile, Soviet leaders regularly charge that the US counterforce weapons (Minuteman III, Tridents, Pershing IIs, MX) amount to a growing first-strike threat against the USSR. They also remember the years of US nuclear superiority in the 1950's when some American political and military leaders blatantly advocated a pre-emptive strike.

Whatever the intentions of government leaders, there is mounting evidence of genuine fear and suspicion in each country of first-strike plans on the other side. We believe that the technical characteristics of counterforce weapons—power, speed, unprecedented accuracy—understandably tend to escalate fear and suspicion. Such fear and suspicion are compounded by current efforts to develop space-based "defenses" that, if truly effective, could provide a cover for launching an offensive first strike. We shall evaluate these efforts, below, in the section on Strategic Defense (page 49).

The Idolatry of Deterrence

For forty years the moral function of deterrence doctrine has been to justify the threatened use of nuclear weapons and an unending arms race. We have already indicated in a preliminary way our opposition to any use of nuclear weapons. We have said that the just-war tradition does more to discredit deterrence doctrine than to support it. We have discerned a lack of coherence in deterrence. We have rejected the nuclear idolatry that presumes the power of ultimate judgment and destruction of other nations.

We do not doubt that the threat of nuclear retaliation can be, and has been, a factor inhibiting the resort to nuclear weapons. Fear is a powerful human motive—although its effects are notoriously unpredictable. Deterrence of some sort seems to operate in most institutional and corporate behavior, including the family, education, law enforcement, and church discipline. But we remain profoundly troubled by the military extremities, which deterrence doctrines have legitimized if not motivated.

Deterrence has too long been reverenced as the unquestioned idol of national security. It has become an ideology of conformity too frequently invoked to disparage dissent and to dismiss any alternative foreign policy proposals. In its most idolatrous forms, it has blinded its proponents to the many-sided requirements of genuine security. There can be no unilateral security in the nuclear age. Security has become indivisible. Our vulnerability is mutual. Our security must be mutual. Security requires economic strength and stability, environmental and public health, educational quality, social well-being, public confidence, global cooperation. In short, the indispensable moral qualities of security must not be forfeited to an uncontrolled arms race.

Whatever claims may be made for deterrence policies since 1945, the future is shadowed by the perilous trends of recent years: escalation of the arms race, the spread of nuclear-weapons technologies to other states, the specter of terrorist movements with nuclear bombs, and the unresolved political conflicts in nuclear-prone regions like the Middle East, the Persian Gulf, South Asia, East Asia, and South Africa. Even if it could be proved, as it cannot, that deterrence has had some short-term benefits for several decades, the longer-term consequences of nuclear policies since 1945 threaten to make human survival increasingly precarious.

Some Christian leaders have sought to justify deterrence as an interim ethic while nuclear-weapon states pursue arms reduction. As we have seen, Pope John Paul II offered such an interim ethic in his 1982 UN statement: Deterrence "may still be judged morally acceptable" as a step toward "progressive disarmament."

We believe, however, that the moral case for nuclear deterrence, even as an interim ethic, has been undermined by unrelenting arms escalation. Deterrence no longer serves, if it ever did, as a strategy that facilitates disarmament.

Counterforce, or the "countervailing strategy" for the current "modernization" of nuclear weapons, is offered as a kind of "new morality" of deterrence. But the weapons being developed in its name increase first-strike powers and lead to the escalation of mutual suspicion. Their very development, which is projected over long periods of years and even decades, tends to defer any hope of significant disarmament to yet another generation.

We believe the churches of nuclear-weapon states must be sensitive to the charge of inequality and invidious discrimination, which nuclear deterrence tends to ignore. If the United States and Soviet Union continue to maintain their rights to nuclear weapons, and even to multiply those weapons, why should other nations not claim those same rights, especially in view of the superpowers' default on their own treaty promises to end nuclear testing and proceed toward nuclear disarmament? If deterrence is good for national security for some nations, why not for other nations? The persistence of such prejudicial conduct bids to become the prime obstacle to effective international cooperation to control nuclear perils.

Nuclear deterrence has become a dogmatic license for perpetual hostility between the superpowers and for their rigid resistance to significant measures of disarmament. Major General Kermit D. Johnson, former Chief of Chaplains of the US Army, in written testimony submitted to our hearing panel, puts it this way:

Before any nuclear weapons are ever launched, nuclear deterrence locks us into a permanent state of war, albeit a cold war, with the Soviet Union. They are regarded as an "enemy," imminently deserving of being threatened moment by moment with nuclear destruction. The overall political relationship between the US and the Soviet Union is fixed by this military reality.

This primary reliance on unrelenting terror tends to perpetuate the most distorted and inhuman images of our "enemy." It forsakes the more prudent, positive strategies of offers, inducements, and incentives that might draw on the vast human, economic, and technological resources of the US and its allies.

We believe there is a still more fundamental flaw at the very core of deterrence doctrine: a contradiction between inordinate confidence in the rationality of decision makers and the absolute terror of annihilation. Nothing in our understanding of fallible and fallen human nature warrants the expectation that this relentless strain between reason and terror can endure indefinitely. The foundations of an enduring peace must be constructive and cooperative.

The rejection of nuclear deterrence, however, does not necessarily mean immediate, unilateral disarmament. Those who regard themselves as nuclear pacifists do not hold a fully responsible position if they only say No to nuclear weapons; they must also share in the difficult political task of working out a strategy of phased arms reductions.

It is the idolatrous connection between the ideology of deterrence and the existence of the weapons themselves that must be broken. Deterrence must no longer receive the churches' blessing, even as a temporary warrant for the maintenance of nuclear weapons. The interim possession of such weapons for a strictly limited time requires a different justification— an ethic of reciprocity as nuclear-weapon states act together in agreed stages to reduce and ultimately to eliminate their nuclear arms. Such an ethic is shaped by an acceptance of mutual vulnerability, a vision of common security, and the escalation of mutual trust rather than mutual terror. It insists that the positive work of peacemaking must overcome the fearful manipulation of hostility.

We believe that neither the US nor any other nuclear power can extricate itself unilaterally from all nuclear perils. Indeed, immediate and total nuclear disarmament by the US might well tempt other countries to develop or expand their own nuclear arsenals, thereby increasing the risk of nuclear war. Whatever the objective truth about the effects of deterrence, faith in that doctrine will not die quickly. It will take prudent political leadership in partnership with all other nuclear-weapon states, including "enemies," to conceive and implement step-by-step approaches to disarmament. Prudence is always a moral obligation. In Chapter 5, we propose several transitional measures toward the goal of a nuclear-free world.

Strategic Defense: Alternative to Deterrence?

For most of the post-Hiroshima years, major governments and military strategists have assumed that nations are defenseless against nuclear weapons. In the ABM (Anti-Ballistic Missile) Treaty of 1972, the superpowers acknowledged this mutual vulnerability and virtually abandoned confidence in the technical prospects for nuclear defenses.

On March 23, 1983, President Reagan dramatically sought to revive hopes for defensive technologies. He proposed an ambitious program of research to make nuclear weapons "impotent and obsolete." That program, termed the Strategic Defense Initiative (SDI) and unofficially called "Star Wars," has rapidly moved from a presidential dream to congressional funding to a crucial factor in the resumed US-Soviet negotiations in Geneva.

We have been presented with much earnest testimony on this issue. Some SDI advocates view the program as a humane alternative to the "immorality" of deterrence. As the enormity of the technological problems has been more fully exposed and SDI planners have had to confront widespread criticism from scientists, official expectations have been stated more modestly.

Brigadier General Robert R. Rankine, Jr., a United Methodist layman serving as the US Air Force Special Assistant for SDI, testified to our hearing panel that SDI "could provide an alternative to reliance on offensive nuclear retaliation as the sole basis for strategic deterrence, and lead to the ultimate goal of eliminating the threat of ballistic missiles."

On this, as on many technical issues, we cannot as bishops

claim to have the expertise to make an authoritative judgment. However, we feel compelled to raise a number of questions that reach beyond purely technical considerations. We are convinced that the moral and political dimensions of this new quest for nuclear defenses are understandable to nonexperts and must be made understandable for our church people.

We observe, first of all, that the moral promise of SDI seems to have shifted from replacing deterrence to "enhancing" deterrence. The result, we believe, is a dangerous new confusion about the relationship between defense and offense in US nuclear policy. There have also been confusing and contradictory claims about the kinds of weapons proposed: whether they will actually protect people or only protect missiles; whether they will be non-nuclear or require nuclear-weapon components; whether they will be space-based or ground-based, or both. We shall note several implications of this confusion below.

If we ourselves cannot evaluate the myriad of new technologies at stake in the SDI program, we do note what appears to be an overwhelming skepticism among US scientists not directly employed in aerospace industry. Cornell University astrophysicist Carl Sagan, a longtime government consultant in space science, told our hearing panel that SDI represents an untestable combination of technologies and a "dangerous and foolish" technical fix on problems that are essentially political: US-Soviet relations. The simple arithmetic of SDI effectiveness is deeply discouraging. If US strategic defenses prove 99 percent effective against 10,000 incoming nuclear warheads, the mere 1 percent that penetrated—100 warheads—could still obliterate most US cities. It has also become apparent that SDI's defenses, at their best, could not cope with low-flying cruise missiles or aircraft or with smuggled weapons. Cities would be the most vulnerable targets of nuclear weapons on both sides, thus increasing rather than removing the threat to population centers.

On the other hand, if SDI should seem to promise a perfect shield, this "defense" would have provocative *offensive* implications, no matter what US leaders say about their intentions. A foolproof defense would indeed make an adversary's deterrent forces "impotent," thus heightening insecurity and raising fears of a possible US first strike—a pre-emptive attack with military impunity. Moreover, some space-based weapons (such as lasers) would clearly have offensive as well as defensive capabilities. We therefore reject claims that such "defensive" weapons are more moral than other weapons.

But we doubt that the Soviet Union would tolerate the deployment of such a system. If Soviet leaders begin to suspect that the US mix of offensive and defensive systems threatens them with the prospect of a first strike—however mistaken that suspicion may be—we can imagine they will be increasingly determined to develop new offensive systems to defeat space-based defenses. We do not find credible the Administration's claim that SDI will offer the Soviet Union new incentives to reduce their offensive missile force. Past Soviet behavior suggests that a further buildup is the Soviet Union's more likely response. Ultimately, Soviet leaders may become tempted to consider launching their own pre-emptive strike before their deterrent forces are disarmed by US "defenses." A discovery of that Soviet desperation by US decision makers could well prompt them to contemplate a *pre*-pre-emptive strike on the Soviet Union. Thus the offensive-defensive-offensive dynamics are becoming more and more scrambled and dangerous.

There are several important implications of new space weapons for arms control and disarmament.

President Reagan claims that SDI research is consistent with all of our treaty obligations, including the 1972 Anti-Ballistic Missile Treaty. The White House acknowledges, however, that options to develop and deploy such a defensive system would require treaty modifications.[13] Critics of SDI claim that the clear intent and spirit of the ABM Treaty are already being violated and that the momentum of the program may cause the treaty's demise.

Ambassador Gerard Smith, former director of the US Arms Control and Disarmament Agency and SALT I negotiator in the Nixon Administration, testified to our hearing panel that the present Administration's non-negotiable stance on SDI has become the basic obstacle to any new arms agreement with the USSR. While the USSR is continuing its own space defense research, Soviet officials have repeatedly insisted that a ban on space weapons is a precondition of accords on strategic nuclear weapons.

Not the least of our concerns is the grossness of SDI costs.

Research costs have recently been scaled upward from $26 billion to $35 billion. Former Secretary of Defense James Schlesinger has estimated that production and deployment of a complete space-based defense could cost $1 trillion. SDI bids to become the most expensive project ever undertaken by any government or any other institution, with enormous economic and social consequences. We are particularly disturbed by the blatant self-aggrandizement of some aerospace contractors in promoting SDI's opportunities for profits and jobs.[14]

We therefore commend to all our churches, and to all Christians, the most searching and candid exploration of these disturbing questions concerning the prospects for space-based defense. We are impressed by the doubts of many eminent scientists. We are concerned about the possible offensive implications. We are worried about the consequences for arms reductions. We are appalled at the probable costs. And we remember once again how often the Scriptures warn us against false hopes for peace and security.

Nuclear Weapons as a Justice Issue

Christian peacemaking in the 1980's is everywhere confronted with the demands of justice, especially on behalf of those who are economically and racially oppressed. At times, a painful polarization is experienced between disarmament movements and liberation movements—as if they weren't inextricably bound up together in the struggle for humanization. We believe that the nuclear crisis must be interpreted as a matter of social justice as well as war prevention.

Justice, of course, is the prime concern of the just-war tradition at its highest levels of ethical sensitivity. We have made plain our rejection of nuclear weapons and deterrence according to our interpretation of just-war principles.

Justice is also offended in the double standard by which some nations presume nuclear weapons for themselves while seeking by every moral, legal, and technical means to deny them to others.

Justice is abused in the overwhelming power of nuclear-weapon states to threaten the self-determination, the security, and the very life of nonaligned and nonbelligerent nations because nuclear hostilities are bound to have devastating environmental and human consequences for the whole earth.

Justice is forsaken in the squandering of wealth, now nearly one trillion dollars a year in worldwide military spending, while a holocaust of hunger, malnutrition, disease, and violent death is destroying tens of millions of the world's poorest peoples.

Justice is defiled by the superpowers' implication in conventional arms races and proxy wars in the Third World, causing much present suffering and threatening escalation into a nuclear war.

Justice is denied in the increasing concentration and computerization of nuclear decision making so that the people's rights of participation in matters of their own security and survival are nullified.

The possibilities of nuclear terrorism by revolutionary movements are seriously aggravated by the persistence of such injustices.

Nuclear Weapons and Conventional Weapons

Our attention to the nuclear crisis cannot lead to the neglect of conventional weapons. The linkages between these two classes of weapons are numerous and complex.

Nuclear arsenals have not prevented conventional wars. Some analysts claim that nuclear weapons have "made the world safe for conventional wars," more than 150 of which have occurred since 1945, with tens of millions of casualties. The possession of nuclear weapons has not saved the United States from serious military and political defeats in China, Cuba, Indochina, and Iran.

The costs of conventional forces worldwide continue to exceed those of nuclear forces, although the nuclear portion of US military spending is now rising.

Many weapons systems are "dual-capable"—designed for either conventional or nuclear charges. In such cases as dual-capable aircraft and submarine-launched cruise missiles, the problems of verification of nuclear agreements seriously obstruct progress in arms control.

Our opposition to any use of nuclear weapons predisposes us to favor a "no-first-use" policy for the US and NATO. The Soviet Union made a unilateral declaration of "no first use" in 1982. However, we cannot support the view that NATO would have to undertake a massive buildup of conventional forces before renouncing its option to respond to a conventional attack with nuclear weapons. Such a view is based on two assumptions that appear dubious to us: (1) that the USSR would seriously contemplate an invasion of NATO territory and (2) that Warsaw Pact conventional forces would overwhelm NATO conventional forces. The collective strength of NATO allies, whose ground and naval forces exceed those of the Warsaw Pact; the doubtful reliability of the USSR's Eastern European allies militarily; the technical prowess of NATO's defensive arms; and a lingering Soviet suspicion that NATO might resort to nuclear weapons even after a "no-first-use" declaration all suggest that a major conventional escalation by NATO is hardly necessary.

In our view such steps as a "no-first-use" policy, a withdrawal of battlefield nuclear weapons from Central Europe, and an East-West agreement to reduce or eliminate intermediate-range nuclear weapons would help create a political climate in which conventional force reductions could also be negotiated. To build up conventional forces in pursuit of nuclear arms control may seem superficially to make military sense if one takes the most alarmist view of Soviet intentions and power. But we do not believe it makes political sense. Europe does not need a new conventional arms race that provokes bitter memories of how devastating conventional wars have been for its peoples in this century. Our hope is that Europe and the whole world may find ways to combine nuclear and conventional disarmament so that our common defenses against war itself may be strengthened.

We are even more deeply concerned over conventional arms races in the Third World and their possible escalation into a nuclear war involving the superpowers. While arms exports from the United States and the Soviet Union have greatly intensified regional conflicts in Asia, Africa, and Latin America, other industrialized nations and even Third World countries themselves have become aggressive competitors in the arms trade now totaling close to forty billion dollars a year.[15] The superpowers' interventionary forces compound this problem. Unrelieved injustice, regional hostilities, and nuclear proliferation in the Third World could lead to a catalytic nuclear war into which the United States and the Soviet Union are drawn by their own Third World attachments.

Once again we are compelled to say that increased conventional forces offer no genuine escape from the threat of nuclear war. The war system itself must be overcome.

CHAPTER 3

The Arms Race
and American Society

The nuclear crisis confronts the Christian faith with much more than the primal issues of uranium and plutonium explosives. Every social institution of militarized states has been profoundly affected by the consequent issues—the systemic "fallout" of military technologies and policies. Every society in the world is critically affected, directly or indirectly.

Political Institutions

The nuclear threat has turned sharply inward in its manifold challenges to democratic government.

As Americans prepare to celebrate the Bicentennial of the US Constitution in 1987, they should know that a decision-making time of only a few desperate minutes in a nuclear confrontation has nullified the Constitution's provision in Article I, Section 8: "The Congress shall have power to declare war." But more than the forfeiting of the powers of Congress to the Executive is involved. The President's own authority under Article II, Section 2, as Commander-in-Chief of the Armed Forces is undermined by the reported deficiencies of nuclear command, control, and communications. A number of military officers now have direct access to the codes required for launching a pre-emptive strike, preparations for which have been a Pentagon assignment since the 1950's.[16]

It is not only in moments of nuclear confrontation that the integrity of democratic government is threatened. Four decades of standing military establishments have, for the first time in American history, witnessed the evolution of a web of influence in which all basic institutions are implicated: a "military-industrial-political-scientific-educational-recreational-media-religious complex." Years of such habitual interactions have generated a high degree of autonomy to the bureaucratic momentum of military technology, often with scant regard for the actual state of international relations.

The pervasiveness of this web of influence should warn us against making the armed forces themselves the scapegoats for this militarization of American society. On a number of recent occasions, military leadership has proved more moderate than civilian leadership. The Joint Chiefs of Staff supported the ratification of the SALT II Treaty with the USSR, while the President and the Secretary of Defense opposed the treaty as "fatally flawed." Pentagon efforts to shut down dozens of military installations around the country have been blocked by local interests and their congressional sponsors.

Technology and politics now share an extremely diffuse network. The development and production of strategic weapons systems, precisely because of the complexity of required technologies, can be widely distributed around the country so as to spread their political constituency. Such high tech systems as the MX missile and space-based weapons have enlisted a majority of states and a large number of congressional districts, all with military contracts and subcontracts, for their political support.

We are particularly concerned that this web of influence constantly tends to marshal public opinion on behalf of aggressive foreign policies and extravagant military spending. The multimillion-dollar support of hardline think tanks by some corporate interests has fostered an alarming degree of data manipulation and downright untruths in both the print and broadcast media.[17] Those who work for détente and arms reductions, whether presidents or members of Congress or scientists or religious leaders, often are unfairly and even viciously caricatured as naïve or soft on communism. Too often public debate and elections are dominated and corrupted by the shrill voices of chauvinism, including some "electronic evangelists" who resort to the most extreme hyperboles of the crusade tradition. Unfortunately, the intemperate and self-righteous rhetoric of some peace activists compounds these political difficulties. Truth itself is a constantly bleeding casualty of the nuclear crisis. Peacemaking must be exalted by the churches as a loyal expression of patriotism and honor.

The Economy

In the 1980's the US federal budget has sharply focused the moral issues of national priorities. Military spending has doubled, amounting to $1.2 trillion in five years. That's about $5,200 for each citizen or more than $20,000 for a family of four. Between 1986 and 1990, $2 trillion more is projected: more than $34,000 for a family of four. In fiscal year 1986, military and related spending will amount to more than half of all discretionary spending by Congress, or more than half of all income tax revenue.[18]

The human costs of this buildup in the name of "defense" are borne most directly by those who are actually most defenseless: the poor, the elderly, and the very young, who are the main targets of severe cuts in social programs. US "rearmament" is being purchased with food stamps, welfare checks, rent subsidies, Medicaid payments, school lunches, and nutrition supplements for poor mothers and their children. Half of the nation's Black children live in poverty, as do two fifths of all Hispanic children. More than eight million adults are unemployed at a time of purported "recovery."

The productivity of the American economy has seriously slackened during these same years of high military spending. Not so long ago, the US regularly enjoyed the world's highest productivity growth rates. In the past decade, the US has slipped far behind many other industrial nations, failing to match the competition in more and more product lines, incurring enormous foreign trade deficits, and losing millions of industrial jobs.

We believe that industrial engineering in the civilian economy has failed to keep pace for at least three reasons: (1) the disproportionate allocation of scientific and technical personnel to military production; (2) the commitment of seventy percent of government research and development funds to weapons programs; and (3) the preference of basic US industries for maximum short-term profits at the expense of long-term planning and modernization. Japan is only the most conspicuous example of a nation that, while holding its military spending to low levels, has invested its technological resources overwhelmingly in the civilian economy, thereby dramatically modernizing its industries, innovating products, playing an ascendant role in world trade, and accumulating enormous currency surpluses. Meanwhile, US industries have suffered a loss of efficiency with the aging of machines and facilities and a corresponding loss of competitive prices and quality of goods. It is a sad measure of US economic life at present that only foreign military sales provide a favorable trade category in durable-goods exports.

Even military production itself, however, is more and more revealed as plagued by wasteful management that often defrauds the government, operates without effective competition, and seldom avoids enormous cost overruns.

We believe there is no credible evidence that high levels of military spending contribute to high growth rates in the United States. In fact, the government's own research reports have repeatedly indicated that the civilian economy can generate enough aggregate demand to more than compensate for conversion from military to civilian production. One of the main tenets of communist ideology, especially in the works of Lenin, is that contradictions in capitalist economies drive them to militarism and imperialism. Some American corporation and labor leaders unwittingly take an almost-Leninist line in trying to prove how beneficial military industry is for the economy. We reject such claims. We believe that reduced military spending and conversion to civilian industry could prove extremely salutary to the American economy.

We are strongly committed to restoring the goal of full employment in the United States. We are convinced that, far from helping to solve the problem of unemployment, defense industry is a major part of the problem. Most Pentagon-provider industries create fewer jobs per dollar than the median manufacturing industry. The basic reason is the increasingly capital- and technology-intensive nature of weapons production.[19] Switching military expenditures to the private sector could create hundreds of thousands of additional jobs if the nation made a political decision to do so. The safety of roads and bridges could be greatly improved; deteriorating urban infrastructures might be restored; affordable housing might be created; forests and lakes afflicted with acid rain might be saved; and nuclear and other industrial wastes might be more safely stored.

Race and the Arms Race

The racial dimensions of this struggle over national priorities are increasingly acute. Approximately 40 percent of the US black population are now concentrated in the deteriorating inner core of twenty cities plagued by severe unemployment, unsafe housing, and inadequate health services. Black unemployment in May 1985 was 15.6 percent compared to 6.2 percent for whites. Black teenage unemployment was 40.4 percent compared to 16.1 percent for white teenagers. Even more disturbing is the trend since 1965: a 22 percent increase in black teenage unemployment, with a scant 1.1 percent increase in white teenage unemployment. The continued movement of industrial jobs to the suburbs swells the ranks of hard-core unemployed among minority dwellers in the inner city.[20]

Without a sharp new governmental focus on inner-city peoples, their economy, and their environment, racial polarization is bound to intensify. In testimony to our hearing panel, Congressman Parren Mitchell of Baltimore spoke of the new "contempt for the poor" in the land, suggesting that "if the arms race were to stop tomorrow," there is no assurance that funds would be transferred to human needs. Minority group leaders report increasing awareness of inflammatory code words and diminished action by government agencies charged by law with enforcing civil rights, not to mention official efforts to reverse the civil rights gains of the past two decades. Clearly the demilitarization of America must be accompanied by a powerful new national commitment to equal opportunity and intergroup dependence for racially disadvantaged peoples.

Psychological and Spiritual Dimensions

The consequent issues of the arms race ultimately have an impact on individual human beings. Systems decisively affect persons. Those charged with direct political and military responsibility for nuclear weapons are peculiarly subject to the strain of psychological contradictions—the rational management of weapons of suicidal terror. As citizens become conscious of the inability of their own powerful government to defend them and to curb the arms race, their personal insecurity and sense of powerlessness tends to increase. The technological complexity of military and arms control issues, the fear that only a few "experts" can cope with them, and the suspicion of being manipulated by propaganda aggravate the feelings of impotence. Economic maladjustments and racial polarization, made worse by the arms race, blight the hopes of many families and youth for a secure and prosperous future. Women are disproportionately victimized by the distortion of economic and social priorities of highly militarized states.

It is, however, the overhanging threat of nuclear annihilation with its impact on attitudes and behavior that has drawn the greatest attention among psychologists in recent years. The "nuclearism" that permeates a whole culture is reflected in what psychiatrist Robert Jay Lifton calls "psychic numbing": a simultaneous denial that the nuclear problem exists and a sense of helplessness to cope with it. "Nuclearism" seems to affect some policy makers rather oppositely. For three decades national security policy has become more and more obsessed with nuclear weapons to the neglect of political and economic factors. "Nuclearism" magnifies the tendency to escape into the wonderland of technology, to construct intellectual defenses behind jargon such as "nuclear exchange" and "strategic defense initiative," and to ignore the uniquely human and spiritual capacities of persons.

As bishops with pastoral responsibility for the whole church, we seek especially to underscore the consequences of "nuclearism" for families and for children. In testimony to our hearing panel, Washington psychiatrist Justin A. Frank pointed to a surprising contradiction. At the very time that anxiety about the arms race seems to have become a forbidden topic among many adults in a kind of "re-emerging Victorianism," field research indicates that the vast majority of children know about the consequences of nuclear war by the time they enter junior high school. A majority of teenagers rate the threat of nuclear war so highly that they do not expect to live out their normal life span. For parents and children to be unwilling or unable to communicate about such fears is a pastoral challenge of greatest importance.

In a United Methodist confirmation class on Long Island, all of the fifteen- and sixteen-year-olds reacted with fear and shock when asked how real the threat of nuclear war was to them. The pastor reported: "It was as if I had dragged up a deep, dark secret and confronted them with it. Each one felt it would happen in their lifetime. . . . None of the youth believed the government was truthful."[21]

There is a deep-seated fear of "futurelessness" among many people. Some young parents agonize over the question of bringing children into such a world. Student vocational choices seem increasingly bounded by technical fixes and careerist anxieties, which are reinforced by educational pressures at all levels. Adolescent responses include "living in the fast lane" as if there is no tomorrow, cults, drug dependence, despair, and increasing suicide.

For young people and for all Americans, the legitimate need for self-respect as a nation must be lifted above the relentless barrage of aggressive, competitive, and chauvinistic sentiments that assault them not only in political rhetoric but also in commercial, recreational, and even educational institutions. The film and television industries' increasing resort to productions that promote suspicion, animosity, and contempt toward the Soviet Union must be challenged by our churches.

There is a powerful and more hopeful alternative theme in the struggle for nationhood: Working for peace and disarmament is working to strengthen the nation, its resources, its security, and its very soul. There is a heritage of humane values from earlier generations of Americans— values like fairness, pluralism, compassion, generosity, internationalism, rallying to the disadvantaged, a readiness to overcome past enmities, a respect for the rule of law and for peaceful change. Such values help nurture the spirit of reconciliation and the works of peacemaking. They could become once again the main marks of American nationhood.

These domestic burdens of the arms race weigh heavily on other nations as well. The prospects for political liberalization, economic progress, and social well-being for the peoples of the Soviet Union are tragically diminished by the enormous investment of their government in the military sector. The economic and social development of some of the world's poorest countries are distorted and constrained by inordinate arms expenditures and repressive military establishments.

CHAPTER 4

The Arms Race
and World Community

Our consciousness of all the peoples of earth as one whole human family has been vivified for our generation as never before by the emergence of both global threats and global bonds. The nuclear crisis is not primarily a matter of missiles; it is a crisis of human community. We turn our attention now to the US-Soviet conflict, not because we view it as intrinsically more important than all other international relationships, but because we view it as the most serious stumbling block to a peaceable and survivable world community.

The US-Soviet Conflict

The United States and the Soviet Union share the capacity to annihilate each other and the whole human family—not once, but many times. The American and Soviet peoples also share a common humanity, a common aversion to war, a common horror of nuclear weapons, and a common hope for their economic and social well-being.

We are not convinced that revolutionary ideology dominates either Soviet leaders or citizens in the 1980's or that it should be perceived as the primary cause of superpower rivalry. Anticommunist absolutism in the West obscures the deeper reality of Russian and other Soviet nationalisms as well as a widely noted spiritual void among Soviet peoples, especially young adults, which no ritual invocations of "Marxism-Leninism" can begin to fill. Moreover, the absolute identification of Christian faith with capitalism obscures the reality of mixed economies and is an intolerable idolatry.

Nevertheless, there are profound differences between these two nations that are bound to provide conflict and competition for years to come. The Soviet Union has had no governmental experience of democratic liberties in the Western individualistic tradition. Soviet definitions of human rights tend to emphasize economic and social security. The Soviet Union remains an authoritarian state, obsessed with secrecy, repressive of most forms of public protest, overbearing and sometimes brutal in its attempts to dominate states along its borders. However, the murderous purges and personality cult of the Stalin years have long since given way to an uneven pattern of semiliberalization and renewed repression.

Whatever the resentments of Soviet citizens toward their government, they seem strongly united in their national pride; in what their economy and living standards have attained through much hard and sacrificial labor; in their spectacular feats of industrial engineering and space technology; and in the impressive achievements of their art, architecture, music, and literature. They are conspicuously united in their passion for peace—but a peace based on a determination not to be militarily inferior to any other nation. That determination is fortified by bitter memories of ancient and modern invasions and merciless wars that have slaughtered millions and scorched the earth. Nothing in American experience can match the scale of Russian suffering. Perhaps seventy-five million people have died unnatural deaths in the wars, famines, and purges of the Soviet people since 1914.

What particularly intensifies the nuclear crisis is the constant and extreme magnification of USA-USSR differences to the point of demagoguery and even utter dishonesty. For years American presidents and diplomats have testified that this unending manipulation of anti-Soviet emotions is the main hindrance to constructive negotiations. Ambassador James Leonard, former US representative to the Geneva-based Committee on Disarmament, observes:

> The root of our problem in negotiating disarmament agreements is not the particular international framework or approach—whether it's done by treaty or formal talks or whatever. It's more fundamentally in our way of looking at our relations with the Soviet Union and with the world at large. It is, in particular, the extraordinary strength and resiliency of anti-Soviet sentiment in this country. . . . It has a particularly pernicious form,

because it has become clearer and clearer to the leaders of the two parties . . . that . . . the issue of our relations with the Soviet Union, and the question of nuclear war and conventional strength are extremely useful issues when it comes to running for president.[22]

The dean of Soviet affairs specialists in the United States and the former ambassador to the USSR, George Kennan, has highlighted the many moral dimensions of this relentlessly hostile and false depiction of the Soviet Union as "the enemy"—and he has done so in one long, powerful sentence:

This endless series of distortions and oversimplifications; this systematic dehumanization of the leadership of another great country; this routine exaggeration of Moscow's military capabilities and of the supposed iniquity of Soviet intentions; this monotonous misrepresentation of the nature and the attitudes of another great people—and a long-suffering people at that, sorely tried by the vicissitudes of this past century; this ignoring of their pride, their hopes—yes, even of their illusions (for they have their illusions, just as we have ours; and illusions, too, deserve respect); this reckless application of the double standard to the judgment of Soviet conduct and our own; this failure to recognize, finally, the communality of many of their problems and ours as we both move inexorably into the modern technological age; and this corresponding tendency to view all aspects of the relationship in terms of a supposed total and irreconcilable conflict of concerns and of aims: these, believe me, are not the marks of the maturity and discrimination one expects of the diplomacy of a great power; they are the marks of an intellectual primitivism and naïvety unpardonable in a great government.[23]

The history of US-Soviet relations since 1917 has been marked by many unfortunate episodes that might have been avoided had wiser policies prevailed. Each government has given the other abundant cause for grievance. Examples on the US side: landing US troops on Soviet soil in 1918 in a misconceived allied effort to crush the revolution; unwillingness to recognize the Soviet government for fifteen more years; refusal to join the League of Nations and make common cause against Nazi, Italian, and Japanese aggression in the 1930's; refusal of the 1945 Soviet request for a $6 billion loan for postwar reconstruction at a time when most of Soviet Europe was a wasteland and twenty-five million survivors were homeless; prevarication about U-2 overflights of Soviet territory, which led to the collapse of the Eisenhower-Khrushchev summit in Paris in 1960; failure to ratify the SALT II Treaty negotiated by three administrations and regarded by both governments as "the centerpiece of détente."

Examples on the Soviet side: the Communist coup in democratic Czechoslovakia in 1948; closure of the Berlin access routes, thus prompting the Berlin airlift of 1948; deployment of nuclear missiles in Cuba in 1962; suppression of the Hungarian uprising of 1956 and the Prague Spring of 1968; prosecution of a relentlessly hostile policy toward Israel since the 1960's, along with support for Arab extremists and harsh restrictions on Jewish emigration to Israel; abuse of the human rights provisions of the Helsinki Final Act of 1975; degradation of détente by deploying new nuclear missiles in Eastern Europe in the late 1970's; invasion of Afghanistan in 1979.

Our recollection of these and other episodes suggests that self-righteousness is hardly warranted by either superpower. Moral ambiguities abound in this as in most international conflicts. Christians must avoid the naïveté that results from historical ignorance. We must cultivate a profound sense of tragedy about the suffering that might have been prevented by sounder understanding.

While we cannot detail here all the constantly changing and disputed data of the military balance between the United States and the Soviet Union, we do wish to provide some moral perspectives by noting the following:

1. More than 95 percent of the world's 50,000 nuclear weapons are in the arsenals of the United States and Soviet Union, clearly indicating the primary responsibility of those nations for reversing the arms race.

2. In July 1985, according to the Center for Defense Information, US deployments of strategic nuclear weapons (warheads) totaled 11,466, while Soviet warheads totaled 9,208. "Both the U.S. and the U.S.S.R. are continuing a vigorous nuclear buildup, preparing to deploy many new delivery systems and thousands of new warheads."[24]

3. While the Soviet Union has more intercontinental ballistic missiles (ICBMs) and more megatonnage than the US, the US in 1985 continued to possess more total nuclear weapons, at least 3,000 more warheads on submarines and 2,000 more warheads on strategic bombers, and therefore a more diversified nuclear arsenal.[25]

4. While the Soviet Union has more intermediate-range ballistic missiles (IRBMs) in Europe, US IRBMs (such as Pershing IIs and cruise missiles) can reach Soviet territory, as can British and French missiles; but Soviet IRBMs cannot reach the mainland of the United States.

5. The nuclear weapons of all officially acknowledged nuclear-weapon states outside the Soviet Union (US, Britain, France, China) are targeted on the Soviet Union.

6. A single US Trident submarine with 192 warheads could destroy 192 Soviet cities. A single Soviet Typhoon submarine could destroy 180 US cities.[26]

7. While the US has led the way in many stages of the arms race (A-bomb, H-bomb, intercontinental bombers, nuclear submarines, MIRVs, cruise missiles), the Soviet Union has also been first in several stages of escalation (space flights, ICBMs, ABMs, MIRVed Euromissiles).

8. Every major nuclear buildup by the US since 1950, under administrations of both parties, has been promoted by highly exaggerated reports of Soviet military power, such as the "bomber gap," the "missile gap," and the "window of vulnerability," that have later been exposed as untruthful. At the same time, the Soviet Union has been so relentless in its own propaganda distortions that several of its more promising overtures have been prematurely dismissed by the US as "just more propaganda."

9. The claim that the 1970's witnessed a decline in the US strategic arsenal during a Soviet buildup is a serious falsehood. The US only began to install MIRVs (multiple warheads, or "multiple independently targetable reentry vehicles") on ICBMs and submarines in 1970, an action that led to thousands of additional nuclear weapons in the 1970's. Meanwhile, the US proceeded with the development of a vast array of counterforce technologies such as cruise missiles of all kinds, Mark 12-A warheads, Trident missiles and submarines, Pershing II rockets, and MX

missiles. The Soviet Union's multiplication of warheads by MIRVs followed US developments by about five years.[27]

10. There is now widespread recognition that US arms-control proposals in the years 1981–85 were designed to allow a continued US nuclear buildup, while securing either one-sided Soviet reductions or the propaganda advantage of Soviet rejections. The Administration's "zero option" for IRBMs in Europe would actually have allowed NATO to retain thousands of nuclear weapons while obliging the Soviet Union to eliminate all its new SS-20 and older SS-4 and SS-5 missiles. The START (Strategic Arms Reduction Talks) proposals would have forced deep cuts in the Soviet land-based missile force while allowing the US to proceed with "modernization" of all three legs of its strategic triad: MX (land), Tridents (sea), and B-1 and Stealth (bombers).[28]

We call attention to these matters to demonstrate once again that nuclear issues are not simply technical questions. They involve weighty moral questions: the burden of global responsibility, the capacity to see the other side, simple equity, and truthfulness.

As Christians our capacity to address such moral questions is greatly enhanced by our ecumenical bonds with tens of millions of Christians in the Soviet Union. Those who view that country only in ideological or atheistic terms need to discover that there are perhaps fifty million or more members of the Russian Orthodox Church alone, in addition to Baptists, Lutherans, Methodists, Roman Catholics, and other Orthodox bodies. Two or three million Jews and many millions of Muslims and Buddhists also live in the Soviet Union.

This endurance of religious faith and practice seven decades—and three generations—after the Bolshevik Revolution is one of the most remarkable spiritual triumphs of modern history. Christians in the USSR have had to face more than just official antireligous propaganda. Many priests were killed in Stalin's time. Thousands of churches were closed. Many were reopened during World War II and after. While Article 52 of the Soviet Constitution of 1977 guarantees freedom of worship, government authority limits the number of churches and prohibits the churches from organizing educational, social, political, or youth programs. Churches must register with the government, as must all groups in society. Refusal to do so has led to imprisonment for some Baptist pastors. Political dissent by some priests has also led to their incarceration. Christian laity are discriminated against in education and employment, partly because they cannot be Communist Party members. So these churches bear the marks of martyrdom.

Yet Christian life endures. Soviet churches appear to be renewing their strength in the 1980's with the power of Orthodox liturgy, evangelical preaching, and sublime choirs in their crowded sanctuaries. Despite all official constraints, the churches unquestionably serve as precious vessels of their people's profound longing for peace. It now appears that government realism about the irrepressible vitality of Christian faith has recently led to a more respectful and less manipulative posture toward the churches.

The overwhelming size of the Russian Orthodox Church among Soviet Christians, along with the remoteness of Orthodox spirituality for most United Methodists, invites us to devote special attention to the spiritual gifts we may receive from Russian Christians. Among them:

- ☐ A "whole world theology" in which there is no boundary between nature and grace, for God's presence is throughout all creation and revelation is everywhere.
- ☐ A firm grasp of the Incarnation of Jesus Christ, rich in the mystical power of transcendence, but rich also in physical embodiments to be seen, felt, kissed, like ikons, which are really concrete symbols of relations among all generations and whose visible focus makes them centers of prayers.
- ☐ A lively sense of brotherhood and sisterhood with all fellow Christians.
- ☐ A vibrant Resurrection faith among a people who have known massive suffering and death, so that Easter is anticipated each year with fasting and all-night vigils, then celebrated with an explosive "Christ is risen! Alleluia! Alleluia! Alleluia!"
- ☐ An indomitable belief that both suffering and joy are essential marks of Christian discipleship.

We affirm our 1979 statement endorsing the first joint theological declaration ever made by church leaders of the United States and Soviet Union: the "Choose Life" Declaration of the March 1979 Geneva Consultation on Disarmament, sponsored by the National Council of Churches.

That landmark encounter led directly to an unprecedented series of ecumenical exchanges, study programs, and telecasts. We recall two sentences from the opening paragraph of "Choose Life": "We have been drawn together across the differences of language and culture by our common Christian calling to foster life in the midst of a race towards death. We affirm our unity in confessing Christ as Lord and Saviour." We cannot possibly support any use, or threat, of nuclear weapons against millions of our sisters and brothers in Christ.

The North-South Conflict

If the world's most immediately dangerous conflict is the new cold war between the United States and the Soviet Union, that conflict itself extends to every continent and is a fractious force within many nations. Moreover, preoccupation with the superpower rivalry is a major source of injustice to the world's poorest peoples, whether through squandering of resources, neglect, repression, exploitation, proxy wars, nuclear arrogance, or failure to construct the institutions of multilateral cooperation required for humane development. Such cooperation requires a constant awareness that the majority of the world's nations and population belong to the South or the Third World. It is the superpowers' obsession with their own military might, especially their nuclear arsenals, that has tended to turn every North-South issue of economic and social justice into an East-West issue of military confrontation.

Earlier we pointed to the superpowers' violation of the Non-Proliferation Treaty (NPT), a majority of whose parties are Third World nations that have forsworn any rights to nuclear weapons in a solemn covenant committing the nuclear-weapon states to nuclear disarmament. At the same time, the security and very survival of those Third World nations are at the mercy of the superpowers' nuclear decisions. This simultaneous inequity of being economic have-nots and nuclear have-nots is storing up a reservoir of bitterness with unpredictable consequences. Massive poverty and nuclear imperialism are thus more than coincidental experiences in the countries of the Southern Hemisphere. These inequities are compounded by exports of nuclear technology from the US and its NATO allies to countries that have refused to become parties to the NPT, such as Pakistan, India, Brazil, and Argentina. Such exports have apparently been motivated by both anti-Soviet geopolitics and industrial profits. The NPT is thereby weakened because the incentives to join the treaty have been virtually erased and the present treaty parties have been humiliated. Cries of protest are now punctuated with murmurs of withdrawal from the Non-Proliferation Treaty, which remains the world's most important multilateral agreement to prevent nuclear war.[29]

The conventional arms trade, in which the USSR, the USA, and France are now the leading exporters, has been promoted as an alternative to nuclear options for Third World countries. In practice, heavy arms exports from North to South have aggravated regional tensions, raised nuclear temptations, tended to entrench military dictatorships, intensified repression of human rights, obstructed prospects for equitable economic development, and increased the likelihood of superpower interventions.

The national security policies of the United States have seriously distorted official perceptions of the economic and social issues at stake in the struggles of developing countries, most conspicuously now in Central America. A misplaced ideological polarization spurred by anticommunism tends to idealize private-sector and disparage public-sector approaches to economic development, often resulting in favoritism for corporate interests at the expense of basic human needs. This disregard for the poorest of the poor aggravates social unrest, compounds insecurity, and becomes a vicious circle that tempts the US to rely primarily on military forces to contain revolutionary movements. The unfortunate image of American militarism and imperialism becomes a further spur to revolutionary sentiment and perhaps to seeking arms from communist countries, thus providing the US government with "proof" that the struggle was an anti-Soviet conflict after all. Such self-fulfilling prophecies thus frustrate the prospects of humane economic development, free from the hostilities of the renewed cold war.

In testimony to our hearing panel, Bishop Patrocinio Apura of the United Church of Christ in the Philippines reminded us that the first US overseas war was a brutal conflict against Philippine nationalists for six years between 1899 and 1905. US military bases in the Philippines have served as "springboards for interventionist strategies" in Asia, especially in Indochina. Those bases are now believed by Filipinos to be prime targets for nuclear attack. The Marcos "counter-insurgency" campaign, supported by the United States, was regarded by Bishop Apura as a repressive effort of an oligarchy of a few hundred families allied with multinational corporations to suppress popular demands for better wages and living conditions. Some Christian leaders supporting these demands were arrested and tortured. Some "disappeared." The sudden collapse of the Marcos dictatorship in a mostly nonviolent revolution in early 1986 exposed that regime's isolation from the majority of the Filipino people.

The foreign policy and corporate interests of the United States are confronted with a particularly barbarous conflict in South Africa. Nowhere in the world is there a more blatant pattern of injustice that at the same time is a serious threat to world peace. In defense of the vicious repression of *apartheid,* the South African government has heavily armed itself against both insurrection and attack. While killing and incarcerating black protestors, including church leaders committed to nonviolence, the Pretoria regime has been developing the technological resources for nuclear weapons. We believe Western governments must cease all moral and material support of the government of South Africa and make clear their firm support of full political and economic rights for black peoples.

On a global scale, it is the enormity of military spending that most disturbingly exposes the linkage between the arms race and economic justice. For years the United Nations and its specialized agencies have thoroughly documented and interpreted this linkage in the potentially positive terms of "disarmament and development." A veritable disarmament charter adopted by the first UN Special Session on disarmament in 1978 declared:

> The hundreds of billions of dollars spent annually on the manufacture or improvement of weapons are in sombre and dramatic contrast to the want and poverty in which two thirds of the world's population live. This colossal waste of resources is even more serious in that it diverts to military purposes not only material but also technical and human resources which are urgently needed for development in all countries, particularly in the developing

countries. Thus, the economic and social consequences of the arms race are so detrimental that its continuation is obviously incompatible with the implementation of the new international economic order based on justice, equity and co-operation.[30]

The 1981 UN Study on the Relationship Between Disarmament and Development (the Thorsson Report) put the matter even more bluntly in stating that the world must choose between the arms race and development: "It cannot do both." The Thorsson Report also called attention to "the vital dimension of attitudes and perceptions" affecting, and affected by, the arms race.[31]

The UN's Food and Agriculture Organization (FAO) stresses the rights of people to life and to food, the conviction that disarmament is essential to the liberation of the poorest people from hunger and malnutrition, and the political weakness of those people when their basic human needs are forsaken for the more powerful interests at stake in military spending. Current military spending, close to $1 trillion annually or more than $2.5 billion everyday, is thirty times as great as the world's total of official development assistance from all governments.[32] The military expenditures of the two superpowers alone exceed the total value of world trade in agricultural products. The cost of just one nuclear aircraft carrier exceeded the gross national product of fifty-three countries in 1983.[33]

There are more systemic and structural aspects of this relationship between the arms race and world poverty. Developing countries now purchasing two thirds of the world's arms imports have added greatly to their already heavy burdens of external debt, thus inhibiting their own development and straining international monetary and banking institutions. The 1981 Thorsson Report is proving correct in forecasting that the 1980's would be a decade of "sluggish economic growth," due in large part to global expenditures for military purposes.

Perhaps most serious is the mounting crisis of multilateralism in which both superpowers are defaulting badly on the cooperation required to meet the challenges of global interdependence. The Soviet Union, encumbered with its own military extravagance and economic sluggishness, persistently excuses itself from any major role in Third World development. The excuse is ideological. Since the poverty of the South is alleged to be the legacy of Western colonialism, it is not the USSR's responsibility to overcome it.

The United States has aggravated the crisis of multilateralism by playing an increasingly obstructionist role in the United Nations. For two decades the US has been largely unresponsive to the pleading of developing countries for equity in the terms of world trade, money, and debt; recalcitrant in UN efforts to provide adequate food and health programs; and resistant to UN goals for minimum levels of economic aid. The US alone blocked the consummation of the Law of the Sea Treaty that had been an inspired triumph of multilateral diplomacy and bipartisan politics and had promised a practical approach to the common heritage of humanity—with great potential benefits to both developed and developing countries. In both the 1978 and 1982 UN Special Sessions on Disarmament, the US was unwilling to support any practical measures that would recognize the critical linkages between disarmament and development.

We find such conduct unworthy of the strong early heritage of US leadership in the United Nations and of generous humanitarian response to critical needs. The burdens of interdependence call increasingly for common institutions, shared sovereignty, and supranational authority. A new vision of a just and peaceable human family imbued with the loving-kindness of our Creator, a vision that knows the nations now share only one earth, that recognizes the world now has only one choice—the arms buildup or the buildup of community—must inspire our people and our leaders to play an imaginative and constructive part in the defense of creation.

CHAPTER 5

Policies for
a Just Peace

We have drawn sharp contrasts between present foreign policies and our vision of a just and peaceable world community. We know that even the partial realization of such a vision requires a protracted and difficult struggle. But hope abides. We believe the paths to peace remain open.

Here we set forth those policy alternatives that may best express our own principles of peacemaking. We do so knowing that our knowledge is incomplete, that some Christians will conscientiously hold contrary positions, and that fuller understanding and changing historical circumstances may soon cause us to revise our own recommendations.

Toward a Nuclear-Free World

The necessity of reconstructing USA-USSR relations is the crux of the nuclear crisis and an imperative of justice to all earth's peoples. That reconstruction involves developing a regular and systematic pattern of consultation, perhaps including an annual summit conference, between the highest political and military leaders of both countries. It requires a recommitment to substantial scientific, educational, and cultural exchanges.

The policies of reconstruction already have a sound if almost forgotten basis in a USA-USSR agreement negotiated a quarter of a century ago. On September 20, 1961, these two governments signed the Joint Statement of Agreed Principles for Disarmament Negotiations, known as the McCloy-Zorin Agreement. That Agreement coincided with the creation of the US government's Arms Control and Disarmament Agency and facilitated the Limited Nuclear Test Ban Treaty of 1963.

We urge the churches to rediscover the McCloy-Zorin Agreement and to press for government fidelity to it. It was endorsed unanimously by the United Nations General Assembly on December 20, 1961, and has guided UN deliberations on how best to achieve the Agreement's stated goal of general and complete disarmament. The Agreement is both visionary and prudent. It provides for a sequence of stages "within specified time limits," adequate verification and review, equitable balance, and eventual reductions to domestic police forces and an international peace-keeping force. Christians should not lose sight of the Agreement's practical wisdom about the requirements of transition to a peaceable world.

The particular measures we now commend are transitional policies in keeping with the principles of the McCloy-Zorin Agreement. The technical details of particular arms accords are less important than the political achievement of such accords and the direction in which they point. We believe the churches should be prepared to support any one or combination of the following four measures, whichever gives greatest promise of ending the new cold war and reversing the arms race:

1. *Comprehensive Test Ban to Inaugurate a Nuclear Freeze.* We support the completion at long last of a treaty banning all nuclear weapons testing. This action would redeem the solemn pledge of the 1963 Limited Test Ban Treaty and consummate two decades of nearly successful negotiations suspended in 1982. Such a treaty, perhaps more than any other step, would vindicate and strengthen the Non-Proliferation Treaty and thus help to curb the spread of nuclear weapons. It would do much to halt the development of new nuclear weapons. It is the most concrete step to implement a nuclear freeze, which The United Methodist General Conference supported in 1984—a mutual and verifiable freeze on the testing, production, and deployment of nuclear weapons and of missiles and new aircraft designed primarily to deliver nuclear weapons. We believe it is an evasive tactic to delay a comprehensive test ban over disputes concerning the verification of the 150-kiloton limit of the much less significant Threshold Test Ban Treaty of 1974. It is the

occurrence of any major nuclear weapons test that must be verifiable, not the exact measurement of the explosive power of weapons, which should not be exploded at all. There is every reason to have high confidence in the verifiability of any major weapons test.[34]

2. *Consolidation of Existing Treaties and Phased Reductions.* We support an unequivocal reaffirmation of both the purposes and provisions of the ABM Treaty of 1972. Such action would help curb the costly, provocative, and illusory development of new "defensive" missile systems, whether ground-based or space-based. Such a reaffirmation would also help restore the vital role of the Standing Consultative Commission (established by the ABM Treaty) with its grievance procedures, thus defusing the incendiary propaganda on both sides concerning alleged treaty violations. Some updating of the unratified SALT II Treaty could reestablish the baseline principle of parity from which subsequent arms reductions can most readily be negotiated. We support the earliest possible negotiation of phased but rapid reduction of nuclear arsenals, while calling upon all other nuclear-weapon states to agree to parallel arms reductions, to the eventual goal of a mutual and verifiable dismantling of all nuclear armaments. All existing arms control treaties could be further strengthened by accords renouncing research and development of all weapons whose actual deployment is banned by those treaties.

3. *Bans on Space Weapons.* We support agreements banning both offensive and defensive weapons, which now threaten the increasing militarization of space. A ban on the further testing and development of antisatellite (ASAT) weapons would help to restore confidence in the satellite systems that monitor arms treaties and control the deployment of military forces. The USSR stopped testing of a rudimentary ASAT system in 1982 and declared a unilateral moratorium as an incentive to negotiations. A ban on space-based "defenses," as we suggested in Chapter 2, would forestall their offensive and even first-strike implications, reinforce the ABM Treaty, facilitate negotiations on offensive force reductions, and avert what could become the most costly and most illusory weapons system ever produced.

4. *No-First-Use Agreement.* While we oppose any use of nuclear weapons, we support, as a transitional measure, a no-first-use policy by the United States and urge its reinforce-

ment in an agreement with other nuclear-weapon states. The USSR unilaterally announced its own no-first-use policy in 1982, having previously insisted on a bilateral agreement. Such an agreement should be accompanied by the withdrawal of all battlefield nuclear weapons from forward defense areas and also by assurances that no conventional force buildups are preconditions of such a policy.

Implicit in these measures is our opposition to all of the following dangerous trends in the arms race:

☐ All the major offensive counterforce weapons that both superpowers have developed in the past decade. On the US side, we oppose any further production or deployment of MX missiles, Trident submarines and missiles, and Pershing II missiles because their technologies all have first-strike implications. We are equally opposed to such Soviet counterforce weapons as SS-18 and SS-19 land-based missiles, Typhoon submarines and missiles, and SS-20 intermediate-range missiles.

☐ All efforts to achieve nuclear superiority—a meaningless goal, but an exceedingly perilous pursuit.

☐ All strategies designed to promote confidence in the feasibility of a "limited" nuclear war or "prevailing" in such a war.

☐ All weapons systems that, by holding out false hopes of effective defenses against nuclear weapons, actually aggravate the arms race.

We believe a political climate more conducive to negotiations might well be fostered by independent US or Soviet initiatives such as the following:

☐ A moratorium on nuclear tests for a specified period.

☐ A halt in production of fissionable materials for weapons purposes.

☐ A halt in flight tests of strategic weapons.

☐ A decision not to proceed further with a new weapons system such as MX or sea-launched cruise missiles or the B-1 bomber, with projected funds transferred to economic development.

Any such initiative would be an invitation to reciprocal national restraint (RNR), a diplomatic strategy successfully used by Presidents Eisenhower, Kennedy, and Nixon to promote negotiations.[35] Recent Soviet restraints unfortunately have not met with positive US responses.

We have repeatedly called attention to injustices in the

implementation of the *Non-Proliferation Treaty* of 1970. Joint USA-USSR measures of significant nuclear arms control will do more than any other actions to restore the multilateral commitment required to curb the spread of nuclear weapons. But other actions are also needed, including: (1) firmer restrictions on nuclear trade with nations not party to the NPT; (2) effective incentives for persuading nonparties to become parties so that the treaty may approach the goal of universal adherence; and (3) more generous financial support of the International Atomic Energy Agency (IAEA) so that it may more confidently monitor compliance with the NPT. Curbing the perils of nuclear terrorism by revolutionary movements requires more than technical safeguards; it demands a prudent and humane strategy for removing the root causes of terrorism.

We urge the resumption of serious negotiations to reduce conventional arms, including mutual force reductions in Europe and the arms trade in the Third World.

While this study has not devoted major attention to the dismal subject of *chemical and biological weapons,* we are categorically opposed to their production, possession, or use. We therefore urge that treaties outlawing such weapons be reaffirmed and strengthened.

Common Security for the World Community

Our United Methodist Social Principles statement declares: "God's world is one world. . . . We pledge ourselves to seek the meaning of the gospel in all issues that divide people and threaten the growth of world community." In the "guiding principles for a theology for a just peace" in Chapter 1, we said: "The transformation of our conflict-ridden nation-state system into a new world order of common security and interdependent institutions offers the only practical hope for enduring peace."

This vision of the common security of a peaceable world community, grounded in the Scriptures and made vivid by prophets and poets through the centuries, was given legal form in the Charter of the United Nations. The Charter's framework of collective security; peaceful settlement of disputes; and international cooperation in overcoming economic, social, cultural, and humanitarian problems remains the indispensable foundation for building the institutions of common security and interdependence. Whatever the limitations in its present operations, the United Nations' main obstacle to fulfillment is the arrogant refusal of the world's major military and industrial powers to redeem their Charter commitment to make the UN the "center for harmonizing the actions of nations" in the attainment of peace and security.

The UN foundation must be strengthened by more effective means of sharing sovereignty under supranational authority. The McCloy-Zorin Agreement provided for development of a UN peace-keeping force and an international disarmament organization for the inspection and control of armaments. We urge a renewed attention to these institutional requirements of common security, along with new instruments of fact-finding, arms verification, mediation of disputes, and planning for conversion from military to civilian production.

We propose that the inseparability of peace and justice be made manifest in truly substantial *disarmament funds for development*. Such funds, whether based on voluntary contributions or raised through "disarmament dividends" from reductions in military spending, would be devoted to those economic activities of the United Nations most effectively aimed at the basic human needs of the world's poorest peoples.[36]

Beyond such reallocation of resources from military to development purposes, the very structures of interdependence require a much more equitable sharing of power and wealth. We support the imaginative evolution of the United Nations into global systems of governance with effective authority to assure common security regarding environmental perils, scarce resources, financial instability, trade inequities, food and hunger, and flagrant abuses of human rights. Only such a broadened view of security can do justice to peacemaking.

Education for Peaceful Alternatives

We believe the prime alternative to hostility and violence is nurture in the ways of peacemaking itself. While peace research and peace studies have made some progress in the past two decades, we would urge a much stronger commitment to these fields on the part of educational institutions at all levels. Empowerment for peacemaking includes:

☐ Cross-cultural study and encounter, especially with those called "enemies."

- A capacity for conflict resolution, including negotiation, mediation, and conciliation.
- Comprehension of the causes of war, aggression, and violence.
- Knowledge of both armaments and disarmament strategies.
- Cooperative strategies for dealing with global problems.
- A capacity for visioning alternative futures for the world community, including alternative security systems.
- Techniques of peaceable political action, including nonviolent direct action.
- A grasp of alternative perspectives on spirituality, ethics, and lifestyle.

We encourage the churches to mobilize support for specialized local, national, and international institutes for peace research and training along such lines. The US Institute of Peace, recently established by Congress, can be a vital center for legitimizing and advancing peace research and training, providing that it (1) develops a broad and pluralistic approach and (2) preserves its academic freedom from domination or manipulation by official policy makers.

We encourage special study of nonviolent defense and peacemaking forces. In testimony to our hearing panel, Gene Sharp of Harvard University reported: "A vast—but neglected—history exists of people who have nonviolently defied foreign conquerors, domestic tyrants, oppressive systems, internal usurpers, and economic masters." Among notable modern examples are Gandhi's *satyagraha* (soul force) in India, Norway's resistance during Nazi occupation to keep schools free of fascist control, Martin Luther King, Jr.'s civil rights movement, and Solidarity in Poland. Every prospect that either military establishments or revolutionary movements might effectively replace armed force with nonviolent methods deserves Christian support.

A different form of nonviolent action is the ecumenical Witness for Peace in the conflict areas of Central America: a contingent of several dozen persons impartially monitoring hostilities and casualties, seeking to discourage violent attacks, and helping to meet immediate human needs. The experience of this nonviolent peacemaking force has led to proposals by Ronald Sider and others for an International Christian Peace Guard that might also witness in such conflict areas as South Africa, Northern Ireland, and the Polish-Soviet border.

In this world of seemingly relentless violence, more and more of which might have nuclear implications, all Christians and their churches are clearly called to join in exploring every possibility of nonviolent means to a just peace. We recall once more that pacifists and just-war theorists share a moral presumption against violence; they have every reason to collaborate in peace research and education and to join in developing a more inclusive approach to peacemaking.

We recognize that both the imperatives of peacemaking and the impulses to violence are to be found in all world religions. We therefore urge educational and religious institutions to develop substantial programs of study, dialogue, and action between Christians and other faith communities in the common quest for peace.

CHAPTER 6

The Church
as Peacemaker

The church of Jesus Christ, in the power and unity of the Holy Spirit, is called to serve as an alternative community to an alienated and fractured world: a loving and peaceable international company of disciples transcending all governments, races and ideologies, reaching out to all "enemies," ministering to all the victims of poverty and oppression. To be an alternative community is not to withdraw from worldly affairs; it is to be at once a model of humane relationships and a base for social transformation.

That normative statement has some empirical reality in the worldwide circle of Christian faith. But it is our shame that the brokenness of the world is evident almost everywhere in the churches themselves—in national and racial separatism, social enclaves, sectarian divisions, ideological hostilities, and even violent conflict. We have hardly begun to imagine what the church as a transnational community offers in proclaiming "the unsearchable riches of Christ" to the "principalities and powers" (Ephesians 3:8, 10).

The United Methodist Heritage

As United Methodists, we have a particular heritage of a "world parish" in our multinational structure, global ministries, enduring witness for peace and world order, and in our participation in the World Methodist Council.

John Wesley counted war as the ultimate evidence of humanity's fallen, sinful state:

Now, who can reconcile war, I will not say to religion, but

to any degree of reason or common sense? . . . What an amazing way of deciding controversies! What must mankind be, before such a thing as war could ever be known or thought of upon earth? How shocking, how inconceivable a want must there have been of common understanding, as well as common humanity, before any two Governors, or any two nations in the universe, could once think of such a method of decision?[37]

Wesley's legacy also includes the insistence that Christians must "join the two so long divided, knowledge and vital piety." Peacemaking must never become simply a matter of platitudinous but ignorant piety. Nor must it ever be restricted to intellectual expertise. Peacemaking is an affair of both mind and heart. Our study of the nuclear crisis has persuaded us that our own leadership requires deeper knowledge and constant study if we are to be credible witnesses to the peace of Christ. But we are equally persuaded that the nuclear crisis demands of all church leaders an unfailing spiritual power for a lifetime of moral struggle. In the tradition of Wesley class meetings, small groups of Christians sharing disciplines of prayer, study, and action can provide centers of such empowerment for peacemaking.

Our commitment to peace has been persistently renewed in such efforts as the Crusade for a New World Order, which, beginning in 1943, enlisted most of the Methodist agencies to mobilize public support for the United Nations; the establishment in 1963 of the Church Center for the United Nations through the cooperative efforts of the Woman's Division of the Board of Missions and the Board of Christian Social Concerns; the 1963 study on *The Christian Faith and War in the Nuclear Age*; the Bishops' Call for Peace and the Self-Development of Peoples (1972-76); the 1984 Episcopal Address; and the adoption by the 1984 General Conference of the statement on *Christian Faith and Disarmament*. We gratefully acknowledge the adoption of similar documents by other Methodist bodies around the world. We commend the reading of Herman Will's 1984 book, *A Will for Peace*, as a highly informative and inspiring account of our peacemaking heritage.

The Peaceable Spirit

The Wesleyan emphasis on personal holiness can be a powerful source of fidelity in peacemaking. We affirm

83

peacemaking as a sacred calling of the gospel, especially blessed by God, making us *evangelists of shalom*—peace that is overflowing with justice, compassion, and well-being. This holiness of peacemaking as a vocation and lifestyle requires the constant nurture of our spiritual, moral, and physical strength.

Peacemaking is ultimately a spiritual issue. Without conversion of minds and hearts, the political systems of this world will remain estranged from *shalom*. The peaceable spirit can face the reality of the nuclear crisis with neither denial nor despair.

Fear is a constant if unacknowledged presence because everyone has glimpsed the specter of the end of all things. But so is anger among us, expressing itself in hostility among persons and nations; and so is guilt over the potential obliteration of earth; and sorrow over the possible loss of all loved ones as well as one's own future. The struggle of sensitive spirits is not to stifle these rumbling pains, but to lift them up before God so that by God's grace and mercy they may be overcome.

Prayer is the armor of the spirit "against the principalities, against the powers, against the world rulers of this present darkness" (Ephesians 6:11-12). To disarm the powers, we must first disarm ourselves before God. Prayer makes us face our own complicity in the world's hate and violence, our worship of false gods, our blasphemous usurpation of God's judgment. Prayer, reinforced by disciplines of fasting and penance, tempers our passions, our indulgences, and our ambitions. Prayer leads us to repentance so that we may become ministers of reconciliation. So prayer humbles. But prayer also empowers. It lifts us up to affirmation and hope, to praise and song. Prayer makes us instruments of a peace that is not our own to give.

Early Christians at daily prayer felt keenly their kinship with followers of the Way in the remotest sections of the Empire. Christianity grew in an inhospitable world where exile and martyrdom were ever-present possibilities. Yet those ancients were confident, as was Eusebius in the fourth century, that "throughout the whole world in the churches of God in the morning at sunrise and in the evening, hymns and praises . . . are [raised] to God." Communal prayer gave these early, marginalized Christians a daily power of connectedness and mutual support.

Christians remain marginalized in most of today's world. In many lands, they live constantly with the threat of exile or martyrdom. The policies of our own government may make us "enemies" to these sisters and brothers in the faith. Our spiritual solidarity must be renewed every day.

Prayer humanizes our enemies, whether Christian or non-Christian, and connects us with them in God's one world. Prayer transforms our perceptions of power, our attitudes toward authentic security, and our ways of settling conflicts and making peace. Prayer prepares our minds and bodies for action.

The Peaceable Family

The nurture of spirituality has its first and greatest opportunity in the intimate community of the family. Loving parents who share a visible reverence for God and creation, who cultivate *shalom* in all the relationships of the home and neighborhood, and whose work and witness in the world shine with moral integrity, are among the most powerful of all peacemakers. How a family demonstrates affection, shares power and responsibility, resolves conflicts, responds to hostility, copes with illness and injury, expresses grief, encourages achievement, conducts its common meals, spends time and money, plans its vacation and travel, forms its political opinions, confronts fears for the future, and worships or fails to worship God—these questions make the family the potential greenhouse of all peacemaking.

We strongly encourage every United Methodist congregation to develop a family life program that exalts peacemaking as its most precious opportunity to "choose life" so that its children and its children's children may live. Choosing life in the nuclear crisis means helping to nurture a realistic but hopeful attitude toward prospects for avoiding nuclear war. A positive if paradoxical guideline for the churches is implied in a 1983 study by Goldenring and Doctor on student attitudes toward nuclear war. "The students who are more worried about nuclear war have better scores with respect to their adjustment and self-esteem, . . . talked more with their parents, . . . and were more hopeful than the [students] who were less worried [that nuclear war could be prevented]." Apparently, the "less worried students" were actually more fatalistic and resigned to the probability of nuclear war.[38]

Congregations and campus ministries would do well to put these findings to work in their own approaches to peace-making.

Christian Education and Peacemaking

Nurture in the ways of peacemaking is not the exclusive task of the churches. Perhaps nothing that Christian education achieves in the study of peace within the walls of the churches themselves can equal the potential impact of peace education in the public schools, libraries, colleges, and universities. We therefore urge all our churches and members to be active in their communities in promoting education for peaceful alternatives for young children, youth, and adults. Where communities are slow or reluctant to develop such curricula, the churches' own pathfinding programs may serve as models for public emulation.

It remains an essential task of Christian education to help the community of faith understand the nature of commitment to the God of *shalom*. Foundational study of the Bible, Christian tradition, and contemporary struggles of the faith around the world constitute the basic curriculum of Christian education for peace. Our congregations should provide forums for understanding and discussing the most difficult, most controversial, most faith-testing issues that public institutions may not be able or ready to handle. Such issues include conflicts of loyalty and conscience, attitudes toward "enemies," ethical perspectives on nuclear weapons, and alternative concepts of economic justice.

There has never been a time when educational resources for peacemaking were more plentiful, credible, and attractive. One of the most hopeful marks of our somber times is the conscientious response of professional educators, communicators, physicians, psychologists, scientists, social scientists, and former military officers and government officials to the educational challenge of the nuclear crisis. Research institutes, resource networks, teaching materials, and information media now exist in abundance to serve those churches and educational institutions prepared to make peacemaking central to their mission. Every United Methodist congregation and conference should designate persons to serve as knowledgeable resource officers for peace education.

The Vocations of Peacemaking

We know how natural it is for persons to be absorbed in their daily work, its struggles, and its compensations. Yet the ministry of the laity remains a largely unfulfilled doctrine in congregational life, not so much in the responsibilities of church management as in public witness in the arenas of work and citizenship.

We plead for a new vocational strategy of peacemaking. Every form of useful work has its own special opportunities for peacemaking. We ask all our people to lift up the ministry of the laity as a vital bearer of *shalom,* working through *vocational guilds* (occupational groups) in ways that are appropriate to each field of work, whether factory or farm, school or shop or studio, hospital or home, office or travel. We encourage our laity to develop academies for studying the tasks of vocational peacemaking.

Public sector vocations in government, politics, the armed forces, citizen lobbies, and the media all merit pastoral support and congregational nurture. All of them include many persons deeply committed to justice and peace. They, too, should develop *lay academies*—centers for group study and reflection on the meaning of discipleship in the world of work and citizenship. Such fields of work too often are victimized by negative stereotypes among church folk. Congregations should provide opportunities for persons in public sector vocations to testify to their own faith and special burdens.

We know that scientists, engineers, and other workers involved in defense industries face difficult questions of conscience. We want our churches to help such persons confront these questions ethically; we urge the churches to provide a supporting fellowship for such persons in whatever vocational choices they make.

We warmly encourage our pastors, theological educators, chaplains, campus ministers, agency staffs, and all other church workers to see themselves anew as peacemakers. Those who serve in church vocations are the primary gatekeepers who can either open or close the opportunities of corporate witness to the things that make for peace. Pastors must know that every aspect of their ministry—preaching, worship, education, counseling, visitation, administration, community leadership—can be an opening for peacemaking.

87

Helping our people heed the Gospel imperatives to love our enemies and put aside the sword is not an optional matter; it is integral to our pastoral care of souls in a warring world. Theological educators must likewise know that every theological discipline has special contributions to make to peacemaking. We encourage our churches at every level to develop and provide adequate support for full-time ministries of peace education and action.

The Politics of Peacemaking

The powers of decision making in the nuclear crisis are not in the hands of clergy or teachers or physicians or farmers; they are in the hands of political and military authorities. Peacemaking is inescapably political. It means changing the policies and perhaps some of the leaders and structures of government. Two opposite tendencies in our churches make political witness problematical: antipolitical prejudices, which keep many Christians out of action, and idolatrous loyalties to special interests and ideologies.

We might take heart from public opinion polls that consistently show that seventy-five percent or more of US citizens believe there can be no hope of either limiting or winning a nuclear war, that both superpowers possess an overkill capacity of nuclear weapons, and that a nuclear freeze should be negotiated with the USSR.[39] However, these views are not adequately reflected in US nuclear policies, in large part because only a small portion of the public is politically active on peace and disarmament issues.

One of the most important purposes of Christian peacemaking is to equip persons for *political ministry*—the positive exercise of their God-given power in the political arena. We affirm two essential means of fulfilling this purpose: (1) personal involvement of United Methodist leaders, lay and clergy, at every level in nurturing political action as an imperative of *shalom* and (2) direct and regular personal engagement of our church members with policy makers in foreign and defense policy. For Americans, it is especially important to be in touch not only with members of Congress but with executive agencies and influential opinion leaders outside of government.

Christian nurture for political ministry should include experiential learning in the connections between faith and foreign policy. Such learning might come from exposure to persons in public sector vocations, knowledgeable scholars, nationals from other countries, and victims of inhumane policies. It should come from opportunities for direct action. It will prepare Christians for public advocacy, responsible partisanship, consensus building, and secular coalitions. It will fortify Christian courage to dissent and to consider prayerfully the possibility of civil disobedience as a last resort when official policies persist in the flagrant abuse of human rights. It will equip Christians for effective use of communications media. It will reach out to people of diverse views. It will help morally earnest Christians expand their perspectives beyond single-issue causes to the necessity for durable alliances among varied causes and special interests.

We shall seek to strengthen our connectional system's connections with political leaders at all levels. All parts of our church, from local congregations to denominational boards and staffs, must share significantly in this work if peacemaking is to be an authentic priority for United Methodists. Our church must develop stronger networks for advocacy, action alerts, and resource sharing. We are committed to work with all the areas, conferences, districts, and agencies of our church to help create a new political climate for disarmament and peace.

Ecumenism and Peacemaking

As United Methodists, we belong to the *oikoumene,* the church for the whole human family. Ecumenism, in all the fullness of baptism and Eucharist, and in common life throughout all the earth, is crucial to peacemaking. Faithful ecumenism begins with repentance for the brokenness of the Body of Christ in the strife and exclusiveness of the churches themselves, especially when they result in suffering and violence, and even in intensification of the nuclear crisis.

We praise God for the World Council of Churches, which, more than any other Christian body, helps us to know that all Christians belong to one Lord, one faith, and one baptism. We celebrate the voice that the World Council gives to the world's poor and most-abused peoples, whose partnership in the struggle for a just peace is the plain imperative of the gospel.

We praise God for the stronger bridges now being built

between churches in the United States and churches in the Soviet Union. While these efforts are difficult and subject to misunderstanding, they point the way toward an unbreakable solidarity across the nuclear abyss. We call upon United Methodists everywhere to pray regularly for our Christian sisters and brothers in the Soviet Union, to study Russian religious life and thought, and to support ecumenical exchanges with Soviet churches.

We praise God for all the ways in which Christians are now reaching out to one another across the boundaries of sect and state. In the unification of divided churches, in councils of churches, in partnerships to overcome racism, and in bilateral dialogues, the work of Christian unity builds the structures of common witness for ambassadors of Jesus Christ our Lord. In Christ's name we shall pray and work unceasingly for the defense of creation and a just peace.

APPENDIX

A Pastoral Letter
to All United Methodists

From your brothers and sisters in Christ Jesus, the Council of Bishops, to all those people called United Methodist in every land: Grace to you and peace in the name of our Lord Jesus Christ.

With hearts and minds open to Christ, who is our peace;

In obedience to his call to be peacemakers;

And in response to the biblical vision of a wholistic peace, *shalom*, revealed in Scripture to be God's will and purpose for all of creation:

We, the bishops of The United Methodist Church, have been moved by the spirit of Jesus to send you a message that we have titled IN DEFENSE OF CREATION: THE NUCLEAR CRISIS AND A JUST PEACE, a message we believe to be of utmost urgency in our time.

This message has been prepared over a span of two years during which time we have earnestly sought to hear the Word of God through the Scriptures. At the same time we have prayerfully and penitently reflected on the continuing buildup of nuclear arsenals by some of the nations. We have become increasingly aware of the devastation that such weapons can inflict on planet earth. We have watched and agonized over the increase in hostile rhetoric and hate among nations. We have seen the threat of a nuclear confrontation increasing in our world. We have been motivated by our own sense of Christian responsibility and stewardship for the world God created.

This brief *Pastoral Letter* is an introduction to a substantial *Foundation Document* that we have produced as the major portion of our message to the church. In our *Foundation Document* we have attempted to state with clarity the biblical basis for our concerns and our conclusions about the issue we are addressing. We have set forth a theology for peace with justice in our time that reflects our understanding of the mind and will of Jesus Christ. This theology for a just peace reflects also our understanding of those insights of both pacifism and just-war theory that speak with relevance to the issues of the present nuclear crisis.

We write in defense of creation. We do so because the creation itself is under attack. Air and water, trees and fruits and flowers, birds and fish and cattle, all children and youth, women and men live under the darkening shadows of a threatening nuclear winter. We call The United Methodist Church to more faithful witness and action in the face of this worsening nuclear crisis. It is a crisis that threatens to assault not only the whole human family but planet earth itself, even while the arms race itself cruelly destroys millions of lives in conventional wars, repressive violence, and massive poverty.

Therefore, we say a clear and unconditioned *No* to nuclear war and to any use of nuclear weapons. We conclude that nuclear deterrence is a position that cannot receive the church's blessing. We state our complete lack of confidence in proposed "defenses" against nuclear attack and are convinced that the enormous cost of developing such defenses is one more witness to the obvious fact that the arms race is a social justice issue, not only a war and peace issue.

Our document sets forth a number of policies for a just peace, including such disarmament proposals as a comprehensive test ban, a multilateral and mutually verifiable nuclear weapons freeze and the ultimate dismantling of all such weapons, and bans on all space weapons. However, the nuclear crisis is not primarily a matter of technology; it is a crisis of human community. We encourage independent US and Soviet initiatives to foster a political climate conducive to negotiations. We urge a renewed commitment to building the institutional foundations of common security, economic justice, human rights, and environmental conservation. And we make appeal for peace research, studies, and training at all levels of education.

This message we are sending to United Methodist people is not meant to be a consensus opinion of our church or a policy statement of our denomination on the nuclear crisis and the pursuit of peace. It is given from the bishops to the church as both a pastoral and a prophetic word. It is *pastoral* in that we as bishops will seek to lead the church in study, prayer, and action related to this issue and this theme, using the *Foundation Document* as a basic resource and guide. It is *prophetic* in that the *Foundation Document* is our response to the Word of God. It faithfully states our understanding of that Word to our world at this moment in history.

Our message is the result of many months of prayerful study, research, and reflection. It is not given to the church with any feeling that it should be the final word on this issue or with the hope that it will silence all contrary opinions; but rather, we are sending this statement to the church seeking the fullest and fairest possible discussion of our understandings and convictions, together with an honest consideration of different and critical opinions.

Peacemaking is ultimately a spiritual issue. It is a sacred calling of Jesus. All dimensions of church life offer openings for peacemaking: family life, Christian education, the ministry of the laity, pastoral ministry in every respect, political witness, and the great fact of the church as a worldwide company of disciples that transcends all nations, governments, races, and ideologies.

Now, therefore, we ask you, our sisters and brothers, to join with us in a new covenant of peacemaking; to use the Bible together with our Council's *Foundation Document* as basic resources for earnest and steadfast study of the issues of justice and peace. We call upon each local pastor and lay leader to give leadership in a local church study of the issues surrounding the nuclear threat. We ask you all to open again your hearts, as we open our hearts, to receive God's gracious gift of peace; to become with us evangelists of *shalom*, making the ways of Jesus the model of discipleship, embracing all neighbors near and far, all friends and enemies, and becoming defenders of God's good creation; and to pray without ceasing for peace in our time.

Now we draw this *Pastoral Letter* to a close with prayers for all of you and for all the nations and peoples of the earth.

We humbly pray that God will accept and use our lives and resources that we dedicate again to a ministry of peace.

May the love of God, the peace of Christ, and the power of the Holy Spirit be among you, everywhere and always, so that you may be a blessing to all creation and to all the children of God, making peace and remembering the poor, choosing life and coming to life eternal, in God's own good time.

Amen.

Notes

[1] We commend the reading of Herman Will's book, *A Will for Peace* (General Board of Church and Society of The United Methodist Church, 1984), as a highly informative and inspiring account of our peacemaking heritage.

[2] From *The Challenge of Peace: God's Promise and Our Response*, copyright © 1983 by the United States Catholic Conference, ¶50-51; page 16. Excerpt used with permission.

[3] From "Dialogue With Trypho" in *The Fathers of the Church: Writings of Saint Justin Martyr*, edited by Thomas B. Falls, D.D., Ph.D. (Christian Heritage, Inc., 1948); page 318.

[4] From *Origen: Contra Celsum*, Book VIII, translated by Henry Chadwick (Cambridge University Press, 1965), ¶68; page 504.

[5] From *Statement to United States Senate Foreign Relations Committee*, by Caspar Weinberger, January 31, 1985.

[6] From *Gathered for Life: Official Report, VI Assembly World Council of Churches*, edited by David Gill (Wm. B. Eerdmans, © 1983 by the World Council of Churches); page 137.

[7] From *Gathered for Life*; page 136.

[8] From *Nuclear Ethics: A Christian Moral Argument*, by David Hollenbach, S. J. (Paulist Press, © 1983); page 83. Used by permission.

[9] See "Nuclear Weapons and the Atlantic Alliance" by McGeorge Bundy, George F. Kennan, Robert S. McNamara, and Gerard Smith in *Foreign Affairs*, Spring 1982; page 753-68.

[10] From "Message U.N. Special Session 1982," # 8, as quoted in *The Challenge of Peace: God's Promise and Our Response* (copyright © 1983 by the United States Catholic Conference); page 54.

[11] *Living with Nuclear Weapons*, by the Harvard Nuclear Study Group (Harvard University Press, 1983).

[12] From *Annual Report to the Congress, Fiscal Year 1986*, by the United States Department of Defense, February 4, 1985; page 45.

[13] See the speech on national security by President Ronald Reagan, March 23, 1983, printed in *Weekly Compilation of Presidential Documents*, Vol. 19, No. 12; pages 442-48. See also *The President's Strategic Defense Initiative*, June 1985, U.S. Department of State, Bureau of Public Affairs, Special Report No. 129.

[14] For further information about the costs and risks of SDI, see "Militarizing the Last Frontier: The Space Weapons Race," in *The Defense Monitor*, Vol. XII, No. 5, 1983.

[15]See *World Military Expenditures and Arms Transfers 1985* (U.S. Arms Control and Disarmament Agency, 1985).

[16]From *The Button: The Pentagon's Strategic Command and Control System*, by Daniel F. Ford (Simon and Schuster, 1985).

[17]A notable example is the disbursement of over $22 million in the 1973-80 period by Richard M. Scaife, heir to the Mellon fortune, to such institutions as the Center for Strategic and International Studies (Georgetown University), the Heritage Foundation (Washington, DC), the Committee on the Present Danger (Washington, DC), the Hoover Institution on War, Revolution, and Peace (Stanford University), and the Institute for Contemporary Studies (San Francisco). See "Citizen Scaife," by Karen Rothmyer in *Columbia Journalism Review*, July/August 1981; page 47. See also "The Conservative Elite," by Sidney Blumenthal, a four-part series in *The Washington Post*, September 22-25, 1985, highlighting the funding of conservative think tanks by the Olin Foundation, the Smith-Richardson Foundation, and Joseph Coors Breweries.

[18]Congressman Parren J. Mitchell in testimony before our hearing panel, July 16, 1985. See also *The Fiscal Year 1986 Defense Budget* (Center on Budget and Policy Priorities, April 1985).

[19]From "The Arms Race and American Society, Impact on the Economy," a statement prepared by Tex Sample for the Committee on Episcopal Initiatives, July 1985. See *Military Expansion, Economic Decline*, by Robert W. DeGrasse, Jr., Council on Economic Priorities (M.E. Sharpe, Inc., 1983); page 29.

[20]From "Impact on Health and Welfare," a statement prepared by Althea T. L. Simmons for the Committee on Episcopal Initiatives, July 1985.

[21]From "Youth Issues of Vocation and Conscience," a statement prepared by Janet Porcher for the Committee on Episcopal Initiatives, July 1985.

[22]From *Nuclear Negotiations: Reassessing Arms Control Goals in U.S.-Soviet Relations*, edited by Alan F. Neidle (Lyndon B. Johnson School of Public Afairs, 1982); page 105. Permission to reprint granted by the Office of Publications, LBJ School of Public Affairs, The University of Texas at Austin.

[23]From *The Nuclear Delusion: Soviet-American Relations in the Atomic Age*, by George F. Kennan (Pantheon Books, © 1983); page 197. Used by permission of Pantheon Books, a Division of Random House, Inc.

[24]From "U.S.-Soviet Nuclear Arms: 1985," in *The Defense Monitor*, Vol. XIV, No. 6, 1985; pages 5, 8.

[25]From "U.S.-Soviet Nuclear Arms: 1985"; pages 3-4.

[26]See *Soviet Military Power 1985* (U.S. Department of Defense, 1985); pages 31-33.

[27]Total US strategic nuclear warheads increased from about 4,000 in 1969 to about 9,000 by 1980. From "U.S.-Soviet Military Facts," in *The Defense Monitor*, Vol. XI, No. 6, 1982; page 3. See also *The Counterforce Syndrome: A Guide to U.S. Nuclear Weapons and Strategic Doctrine*, by Robert C. Aldridge (Institute for Policy Studies, 1978), pages 8-13; the annual publication of *The Military Balance* (International Institute for Strategic Studies); the annual *World Armaments and Disarmaments: SIPRI Yearbook*, Stockholm International Peace Research Institute (Taylor and Francis, Inc.).

[28]Strobe Talbott, diplomatic correspondent for *Time* magazine and former Rhodes Scholar, summarized his 350-page study of the Reagan Administration's arms control policies in his Foreword by noting that the most influential officials in the Administration "questioned the desirability of any agreement that entailed accommodation with America's principal adversary and limitation of America's military options. If forced to keep up the appearance of playing the old arms-control game, they believed, the U.S. would do best with gambits at the negotiating table that would lead to diplomatic stalemate; that way the U.S.

might more freely acquire and deploy new pieces on its side of the board and position itself, if necessary, to make winning military moves against the Soviet Union.

"The Administration's conduct of the INF talks and START brought about an unprecedented crisis in the already strained quarter-century-old arms-control process." From *Deadly Gambits: The Reagan Administration and the Stalemate in Nuclear Arms Control* (Alfred A. Knopf, Inc., © 1984); page xii. Used by permission. See also "Deep Cuts," by Michael Krepon in *Nuclear Arms Control: Options for the 1980s* (The Arms Control Association, 1982), page 57, which noted: "If carried out, START reductions would require significant reductions in current Soviet ICBM forces without requiring the U.S. to shelve any planned strategic modernization programs."

[29]The Stockholm International Peace Research Institute reports extreme Soviet caution and restraint concerning nuclear exports by the USSR. No enrichment or reprocessing technology is exported and all spent fuel is returned to the USSR. From *The NPT: The Main Political Barrier to Nuclear Weapon Proliferation* (Taylor and Francis Ltd., 1980); page 27. See also *Controlling the Bomb: Nuclear Proliferation in the 1980s*, by Lewis A. Dunn (Yale University Press, 1982) and *Nuclear Proliferation: A Citizen's Guide to Policy Choices*, by Ann Florini (United Nations Association of the United States of America, Inc.).

[30]From the Final Document of the United Nations Special Session on Disarmament, July 13, 1978, UN Document A/RES/S-10/2, ¶16; page 6.

[31]From the Study on the Relationship Between Disarmament and Development, October 5, 1981, UN Document A/36/356, ¶391-426; page 161.

[32]See *World Military Expenditures and Arms Transfers 1985* (U.S. Arms Control and Disarmament Agency, 1985); page 3.

[33]From *The United Nations Disarmament Yearbook, Volume 8: 1983*, Department of Disarmament Affairs (United Nations, 1984); page 505.

[34]See the section on verification in "Simultaneous Test Ban: A Primer on Nuclear Explosions," in *The Defense Monitor*, Vol. XIV, No. 5, 1985; pages 10-12. See also "The Verification of a Comprehensive Nuclear Test Ban," by Lynn R. Sykes and Jack F. Evernden, in *Scientific American*, October 1982; pages 47-55.

[35]See "Reciprocal National Restraint: An Alternative Path," by Herbert Scoville, Jr., in *Arms Control Today*, June 1985.

[36]From the Study on the Relationship Between Disarmament and Development, October 5, 1981, UN Document A/36/356, ¶391-426; page 161.

[37]From "The Doctrine of Original Sin" in *The Works of John Wesley*, Vol. IX (Zondervan, 1959 [originally published in London, England, 1872]); pages 221-22.

[38]Cited by Dr. Justin A. Frank in testimony before our hearing panel, July 16, 1985.

[39]From *Voter Options on Nuclear Arms Policy* (The Public Agenda Foundation, 1984); pages 18-23. See also Penn and Schoen Associates, *Poll Findings on the Nuclear Freeze* (a national poll conducted for the Committee on the Present Danger, April 16, 1984); page 4. While the Committee itself has opposed a nuclear freeze, the poll revealed that 81 percent favored a bilateral freeze, 16 percent opposed it, and 4 percent had no opinion.